# SMASHING
# Logo Design

## PUBLISHER'S ACKNOWLEDGMENTS

Some of the people who helped bring this book to market include the following:

*Editorial and Production*
VP Consumer and Technology Publishing Director: Michelle Leete
Associate Director–Book Content Management: Martin Tribe
Associate Publisher: Chris Webb
Publishing Assistant: Ellie Scott
Development Editor: Elizabeth Kuball
Copy Editor: Elizabeth Kuball
Technical Editor: Mike Rock
Editorial Manager: Jodi Jensen
Senior Project Editor: Sara Shlaer
Editorial Assistant: Leslie Saxman

*Marketing*
Marketing Manager: Louise Breinholt
Marketing Executive: Kate Parrett

*Composition Services*
Compositor: Indianapolis Composition Services
Proofreader: Susan Hobbs
Indexer: Potomac Indexing, LLC

# SMASHING
# Logo Design

## THE ART OF CREATING VISUAL IDENTITIES

## Gareth Hardy

A John Wiley and Sons, Ltd, Publication

For Mum and Dad. Without you, this book would not exist.

# Author's Acknowledgments

Many people have been involved in making this book a possibility. I'd like to thank my editor, Elizabeth Kuball, for managing with great patience to decipher my confusing thoughts into coherent English, and Chris Webb for giving me this amazing opportunity. I'd also like to thank Mike Rock for his invaluable advice and Charlotte Morris for being my human thesaurus and official logo tester. I'd like to thank the vast network of staff at both John Wiley & Sons and *Smashing Magazine*.

Finally, a massive thanks to all the designers who submitted logos for the book and to the following people, in particular, for putting up with my questions and for giving me some of their invaluable time:

| | | |
|---|---|---|
| Milton Glaser | Nadim Twal | Galin Kastelov |
| Leighton Hubbell | Oguzhan Ocalan | Sean O'Grady |
| Nav Iqbal | Von Glitschka | Andrej Matic |
| Raja Sandhu | Denis Olenik | Nathan Sarlow |
| Mike Erickson | Jan Zábranský | Stephanie Reeves |
| Glen Hobbs | Josh Hayes | |
| Steve Douglas | Kevin Burr | |

# About the Author

**Gareth Hardy** is a graphic designer based in Birmingham, England. He worked as a senior graphic designer but grew frustrated by the restrictions on creativity in the corporate environment, so he made the daring leap into freelance in 2008.

Gareth's experience and knowledge spans the broad spectrum of graphic design. He has achieved a first-class degree in the field and been employed as a professional web designer. This vast arsenal of design-related expertise allows Gareth the opportunity to advise clients on the complete brand-identity package. He specializes in revolutionary brand-identity solutions for clients of all sizes, both domestically and internationally.

Gareth works under the tongue-in-cheek moniker of Down With Design. He also frequently writes articles related to design that provide a unique take on events. His works and more information about his background are available at www.downwithdesign.com.

# Contents

# Introduction

My first memory of being fascinated by a logo was when I was 4 or 5 years old, around the time my dad first introduced me to my favorite football team. Even at that tender young age, I thought it was great that I could identity with my team of choice by seeing the club crest emblazoned on the jerseys of the players and on the stadium that they played in. I'd ask for the latest replica shirt for birthdays and Christmases, and I insisted that my whole bedroom be adorned with the official crest. The wallpaper, curtains, bed linens, lamp, rug—everything featured the logo.

I even spent time messing around with my own artwork by carefully tracing over a print of the logo I found in a magazine, until I felt confident enough in my own abilities to draw it freehand. These early behaviors practically carved out my career path. The beautiful thing about logos is that they can affect our lives without our even noticing. They have a lasting impact on designers and nondesigners alike. We live in a branded world, and that's not about to change any time soon.

In the years I spent employed as a graphic designer, the task I relished most was designing a logo. To this day, I still find logo design to be the most challenging and rewarding project of any of the different design disciplines that I undertake. It's a great feeling when you know that you've successfully answered a tough brief or made someone else's vision become a reality. My passion for logo design and brand identity led me to leave my full-time position as a senior graphic designer and enter the competitive foray of freelance. As a freelancer, I've discovered that there are thousands upon thousands of talented designers out there, all striving to create the next great logo.

Recently, logo design has almost become its own discipline within the design field, creating a new emerging market. I'm fascinated with exploring whether this shift will have a positive or negative effect on designers. The fact that you've picked up this book means that you have an interest in logos. Maybe you share a story similar to my own. By reading this book, you'll learn what you need to know in order to stay ahead of the game and keep your ideas fresh and original.

This book is divided into three parts. In the first part, you'll learn about the theory associated with logos and gain a candid insight into the ever-changing world of logo design. In the second part, I offer loads of advice on how to create a logo for yourself. Finally, the third part is a showcase of successful logos designed by creatives from all over the world.

*Smashing Logo Design* should not be considered the definitive instruction manual to designing a logo—it's impossible to carve in stone a set of steps that you should follow every time you design a logo. Every designer's process is unique. But in this book, I share with you a routine that I've found to be successful. As a creative individual, you can expand on this process and explore methods that work best for you. When you've finished reading this book, not only will you be inspired, but you'll have a greater understanding of the small image that we call the logo.

# THE POWER OF LOGOS

# 1

# THE LOGO

WHEN I SAY the brand name Nike, what pops into your mind? Odds are, it's the famous Nike Swoosh. What about McDonald's? Are you picturing the Golden Arches? These famous brands are so tied to their logos that you (and billions of people like you) have trouble thinking of the name of the brand without also thinking of the logo. And the reverse is also true: The logo is immediately identifiable with the brand. That's the power of a logo.

A logo is a graphic identifier that is used to visually communicate anything that requires to be identified. It helps the brand set itself apart from the competition—you don't see the Golden Arches and think of Burger King. And yet logos are not limited to commercial endeavors— charitable organizations, campaigns, even individuals can use logos to identify themselves.

In this chapter, I introduce you to what logos are, who uses logos, and where logos are used.

## WHAT LOGOS ARE

So, what exactly is a logo? To answer this question, I sought the opinion of Milton Glaser, one of the most revered designers in the history of graphic design. His most notable logo design work is the identity for the I ♥ New York campaign, which has been in use since its introduction in the mid-1970s. Mr. Glaser has worked with and designed logos for over 50 years, so he seemed like the perfect candidate to ask what a logo is. Here's his definition:

> *A logo is either a series of words or an image that attempts to represent an institution or an individual in a way that is symbolic in some cases or parallels the person's identity. If it's for an individual, the logo is very often for their name itself. On the other hand, some logos are abstract, and others use literature or words to achieve their effect. In any case, what logos attempt to do is synthesize an individual or institution into an understandable visual form.*

An enterprise without a logo has no chance of making an impact on its target audience. You have to be seen to be heard. Logos help to communicate with the target audience and are often the first point of contact with that group.

**Remember:** When a logo is used for a brand, the logo is a *representation* of the brand, not the brand itself.

4

## WHO USES LOGOS

Logos are not just used by massive corporations. A logo can be used to represent just about anything or anyone:

- **Businesses:** In order to create a fully functional identity, most businesses use logos. Logos are everywhere in the business world, from the largest corporations to the mom-and-pop store on the corner.
- **Products:** A business might have a logo to identify itself, as well as logos for each of its products. Or it might use the same logo to identify itself as it uses to identify all its products. For example, Apple uses the same logo for everything it produces, from MacBooks to iPods to iPhones. On the other hand, SC Johnson has a logo to represent the company itself, and separate logos for each of its products, including Windex, Ziploc, and Drano.
- **Individuals:** Some people, like celebrities and sports stars, have become brands themselves. David and Victoria Beckham are the perfect example of celebrity brand power. When they got married, it only magnified their celebrity, and they soon became aware that they could market themselves as a brand. They've recently launched a perfume and aftershave range that features a monogram of their initials, DVB.

  Many celebrities on a similar level have become wise to the power of personal branding to increase their income. Tennis star Roger Federer is often seen on court wearing a hat that features his own personal logo. The same goes for golfer Tiger Woods and many other world famous celebrities.

Of course, an individual doesn't have to be famous in order to use a logo to promote himself or herself. Anyone seeking public recognition of his or her name as an identity can use a logo to achieve this goal.

- **Campaigns:** Any type of campaign that seeks to raise awareness for a cause—whether political or not—uses a logo. Barack Obama's campaign logo—an O filled with a sun rising on the horizon—is an example of a recognizable logo. The same goes for the "got milk?" logo used by the California Milk Processor Board to promote the consumption of milk.

- **Nonprofit organizations and charities:** Just because an organization isn't looking to make a profit doesn't mean that it doesn't need a logo. Charities can use branding power to get people to support their cause.

A logo for a nonprofit organization that made an immediate impact on me was the logo for Live Aid, a music concert that was held in 1985 to help raise funds for victims of famine in Ethiopia. The combination of a guitar and an outline of the African continent really makes you think and helps to spread the reason behind the concert.

## WHERE LOGOS ARE USED

Logos are everywhere:

- **Print:** You can find logos in newspaper and magazine advertisements (see Figure 1-1), on swanky business cards, or on traditional letterheads. Wherever the medium of print is possible, an opportunity to display a logo is there.

Figure 1-1: A printed advertisement for Amazon.co.uk.
Photo by Charlotte Morris

■ **Television and movies:** Logos are used in the commercials on TV, as well as in the advertisements before movies start. But logos aren't just in the commercials—they're in the TV shows and movies themselves. Next time you're watching a TV show or movie, look for logos. Companies often pay to have their products used; this is known as *product placement.*

Some TV shows and movies use fake brands so that they don't have to worry about copyright restrictions or pay to use the real brands, or to set the world of the TV show or movie apart from the real world. For example, Duff Beer is the fictional brand of beverage in the cartoon *The Simpsons.* If you mention the name Duff Beer to a fan of the show or present them with the Duff Beer logo, he'll likely know where it's from, even though it isn't a real brand.

■ **The Internet:** Since it's launch in 1992, the World Wide Web has given brands a new domain (pun intended) to play with. Nearly every company now has an online presence (like the one shown Figure 1-2). The Internet has widened the opportunity for brands to use their logos—it's a new area to compete for visual space.

Figure 1-2: The Shell logo online.
Photo by Charlotte Morris

■ **Signage:** When I first visited the United States back in 2000, the first thing that struck me was the different marketing landscape from what I had been accustomed to back home in England. Driving down the highway at night, I could see a main street in Orlando, lit up with a straight path of signs, each one displaying a different logo. To improve the chances of a passerby glimpsing them from afar, the signs were lit with bright lights, which mimicked their cry for attention, each logo seeking to be more identifiable than its competitors.

This type of logo collage on the landscape seems to have transcended the globe in recent years, with McDonald's signs visible on such structures worldwide (see Figure 1-3). The movie *Logorama* (2009) hints at how logos can take over our surroundings; the events in the film are told through the use of over 2,500 commonly recognizable logos.

Figure 1-3: A common sight across the world.
Photo by Charlotte Morris

# Hiring a logo designer

When embarking on a new enterprise, many business owners are tempted to create their logos themselves, but seeking professional assistance is always a wise move. Finding the right designer can be a daunting prospect, so here are my recommendations:

- Hire a professional. Asking your friend's mom's niece who has dabbled with Microsoft Paint to design your logo may save you money in the short term, but it can have long-term negative effects. Seek the services of a professional graphic designer—someone who clearly knows what he or she is doing.

- Check the designer's portfolio. It's important to assess a potential candidate's track record and experience. Don't be fooled by pretty colors or dummy projects—look for the designer's solutions to real design briefs. If the designer is consistently turning out amazing logo designs, you can be assured that he or she will be able to help you with a new identity.

continued

continued

- Remember that communication is paramount. A good designer will understand your goals and advise you on the best possible route for the project before any work has begun. A good way to judge a designer is to make an inquiry and assess the way he or she approaches your first point of contact. If the designer gets back to you right away with a set price, he or she probably won't have the aims of the project at heart. Each logo design project is different, and the designer's price structure should reflect this—a designer should need to discuss the specifications of the project before setting a price.

- Don't be guided by price. Naturally, your project has a budget, but the cheapest option isn't always the best. Quality doesn't come cheap. There are no set rules for the minimum or maximum that you should spend on a professional logo design, but if a price seems too good to be true, it probably is. **Remember:** A logo is one of the most important investments a business can make to improve its reputation and identity.

- Know your goals. A good designer will design with the sole purpose of meeting your aims and offer you advice along the way. Know what you want, but be open to the advice of the designer—he or she can guide you in the right direction.

# 2

# TYPES OF LOGOS

LOGOS CAN TAKE on many different forms, from pictures to words to abstract symbols. Graphics allow designers to be expressive in a variety of ways. This freedom of expression translates into the logos that you see every day.

Each different type of logo offers advantages and disadvantages to both the designer and the person, product, or organization that the logo identifies. In this chapter, I walk you through the main types of logos and what they're most useful for.

## PICTORIAL MARKS

Pictorial marks are drawings—everything from simple line drawings to detailed illustrations—that use a form of literal imagery as the identifier. Pictorial marks make a quicker connection with the audience through already recognizable images. They often require no explanation, regardless of the language or culture.

The one downside to pictorial marks is that they often require assisting typography to get the message across. That said, some of the larger brands have dropped the typography from their logos altogether. This is becoming a popular trend and one that only helps to simplify the design, in addition to making it more memorable and iconic. As I was writing this book, the international coffeehouse chain Starbucks announced that its logo would be displayed free of type.

Perhaps the most popular and well-known logo that's a pictorial mark is the logo for Apple. Believe it or not, Apple hasn't always used such a clean and literal image to help translate the brand name. The first Apple logo featured a heavily detailed illustration of Sir Isaac Newton sitting under a tree with a single apple hanging from a branch directly above his head, alluding to Newton's groundbreaking discovery of the law of gravity. Steve Jobs, co-founder of Apple, recognized that the logo was far too detailed and wouldn't match the brand image of the company, so he employed the services of Rob Janoff to create a simpler and more iconic mark. Janoff's final outcome (see Figure 2-1) is a clear representation of an apple with the bite mark on the side to help distinguish the image from that of a tomato.

Figure 2-1: The Apple logo, designed by Rob Janoff (www.robjanoff.com).
Photo by Charlotte Morris

Craig Russell, a designer from Melbourne, Australia, chose to implement a pictorial mark for Driving for Charity (see Figure 2-2), a harness-racing charity. The pictorial mark shows this connection between animal and competitor. The simple icon isn't a literal representation, but it also isn't so abstract that it's unrecognizable as an illustration of a horse rider.

Figure 2-2: The Driving for Charity logo, designed by Craig Russell (www.craigrussell.com.au).

Josiah Jost, of Alberta, Canada, designed the new logo for Undersea Productions (see Figure 2-3), an Australian company specializing in underwater imaging. Jost spent some time studying sea life, including footage provided by the company, and noticed the connection between circling fish and an aperture, which, when combined, form the perfect image for underwater photography. The effect makes the viewers feel like they're at the bottom of the ocean, instantly connecting them to the workplace of Undersea Productions.

Figure 2-3: The Undersea Productions logo, designed by Josiah Jost (www.siahdesign.com).

## ABSTRACT AND SYMBOLIC MARKS

Abstract and symbolic marks consist of a nonliteral interpretation of a concept, idea, or belief held by the *identifier* (the organization or individual whom the logo represents). Because they're indefinite, abstract and symbolic marks often rely on geometric shapes, designed with careful precision. Abstract and symbolic marks provide limitless avenues for creativity. They can tell a story. On the downside, abstract and symbolic marks might make less of a connection with the audience because the imagery they employ isn't immediately recognizable. Plus, it's often difficult to find a unique solution that works.

The world-famous Nike Swoosh logo (see Figure 2-4) is perhaps one of the most recognized abstract and symbolic marks. The original logo was designed in 1971 by Carolyn Davidson, who infamously charged only $35 for her graphic design service. The name Nike is taken from the name of the winged goddess in Greek mythology. The simple Swoosh is a symbol of the wing of the goddess, who exemplifies victory; this ties in with a company that originally started as a manufacturer of running shoes. The logo also was meant to inspire athletes to run faster, with the movement it suggests.

Figure 2-4: The Nike Swoosh logo, designed by Carolyn Davidson.

Photo by Charlotte Morris

The logo for Adimurti (see Figure 2-5), a company that sells yoga-related products, was designed by Sergey Shapiro, a graphic designer from Moscow, Russia, who specializes in identity. The symbol evokes a feeling of three people coming together to practice yoga in a calming environment. The mark also could be viewed as a very abstract initial *A*.

Figure 2-5: The Adimurti logo, designed by Sergey Shapiro (www.fromtheska.ru).

Brandberry, an award-winning design company based in Samara, Russia, designed an abstract mark for Idealogy (see Figure 2-6), which is the first official school of strategic communications in social media in Russia. The colorful random shapes within the mark symbolize the fast-paced, ever-changing online world that social media has helped to create.

13

Figure 2-6: The Idealogy logo, designed by Brandberry (www.brandberry.net).

## EMBLEMS

An emblem is an amalgamation of a surrounding shape and the name of the identifier. Emblems can be simple enclosures that capture stylized lettering or intricately illustrated motifs. They're wisely used to help identify sports teams and prestigious organizations (possibly tied to the use of family crests by English monarchs). Emblems help to give people a more personal relationship with the brand, especially if they represent teams or clubs. On the downside, they don't scale well if they're extremely intricate.

Emblems also work extremely well on the packaging of foods. One food product that is well known for its intricate emblem is Lyle's Golden Syrup (see Figure 2-7). The emblem is one of the oldest brands in the United Kingdom. First launched in 1904, the packaging and logo have changed only marginally since, which helps to give the product a brand image of great esteem.

Figure 2-7: The Lyle's Golden Syrup logo.

Photo by Charlotte Morris

Alan Oronoz, an identity designer and illustrator from Chihuahua, Mexico, used a crest logo for Agralot (see Figure 2-8) to create a friendly image, including an illustration of the product that Agralot sells.

Figure 2-8: The Agralot logo, designed by Oronoz Brandesign (www.alanoronoz.com).

John Boerckel, a professional graphic designer working in Philadelphia, was asked to design a new logo for Kennedy's American Barber Club (see Figure 2-9). The coupling of a recognizable image of a pair of scissors with assisting decorative elements drawn in a traditional style instantly makes you think that the barber club is an established organization.

Figure 2-9: The Kennedy's American Barber Club logo, designed by John Boerckel (www.johnboerckel.com).

## CHARACTERS

Characters are more prevalent among institutions and clubs. Businesses that include characters in their logo are typically seen as more fun and not so serious. Characters can invoke humor and remind us of our childhoods because of the cartoon-like illustrative style. A character in a logo can go on to have its own identity and become an official mascot of the company or organization itself. Characters can build strong connections with audiences (especially younger ones), help to support a friendly brand image, and foster brand loyalty. They can be used as the major element in marketing campaigns. On the downside, they might be seen as creating a juvenile brand image, they aren't suitable for every brand. Therefore, the style or nature of the character needs to be chosen carefully.

Monopoly, the popular board game made by Parker Brothers (a subsidiary of Hasbro), has used a character as part of its logo since 1936. Mr. Monopoly (see Figure 2-10), who was originally named "Rich Uncle Pennybags," was introduced to use the power of branding to full effect. Mr. Monopoly—a recognized character that is instantly associated with the product—is still in use today.

Figure 2-10: The Monopoly logo.

Photo by Gareth Hardy

Burn Creative, of Carlisle, Pennsylvania, created an illustrated character for the Carlisle High School Thundering Herd (see Figure 2-11). It serves as the identity for all the school's sports teams. The charging character not only raises team spirit but also just might put a little fear into opposing teams.

Figure 2-11: The logo of the Carlisle High School Thundering Herd, designed by Burn Creative (www.burncreative.com).

Brandberry designed a unique kingfisher character illustration for Alcedo Media (see Figure 2-12). *Alcedo* is a genus of the *Alcedinadae* (river kingfisher) family, and kingfishers are rarely sighted birds. The choice to illustrate the kingfisher character in a modern style helps Alcedo Media to become distinguishable—it's not the type of logo you would commonly associate with a media company, but it's directly tied to the company name.

Figure 2-12: The Alcedo Media logo, designed by Brandberry (www.brandberry.com).

17

## TYPOGRAPHIC

Words and letters can help to translate a message and convey a sense of style in the same way that pictures can. Typographic logos have played an enormous part in the history of logo design. If you look at some of the oldest logos, you'll notice that they primarily utilize type. Some of the earliest logos even had type blocks cut specifically so that they could be reproduced easily. Type can be used in a variety of ways in today's logos.

### WORDMARKS

A wordmark is a logo that displays the name of a brand or individual in a text-only graphic representation. The style of the type can be an existing font that has been tweaked or a custom-designed typeface that has been drawn from scratch. Wordmarks increase the chances of the logo being original, because it focuses on the name of the identifier. Plus, a wordmark can help to form recognition for a new brand name. A potential drawback to wordmarks is that, if they're too simple, their identifiers may struggle for recognition.

One of the world's oldest and most famous brands, Coca-Cola, uses a wordmark for the logo of its product, a carbonated soft drink (see Figure 2-13). The logo was designed by Frank Mason Robinson in 1885 and has hardly changed since, with only marginal improvements made to ensure that it performs well in all applications. The old-school script style of the wordmark adds character and still stands out more than a hundred years after it was first introduced.

Figure 2-13: The Coca-Cola logo, designed by Frank Mason Robinson.

Photo by Charlotte Morris

Mads Burcharth, a type-obsessed designer from Odense, Denmark, designed an elaborate new wordmark for Wallen, a Danish jewelry designer (see Figure 2-14). The flowing letterforms in a classic script style help to portray an elegant and luxurious brand image, which reflects the quality of the products that Wallen offers.

Figure 2-14: The Wallen logo, designed by Mads Burcharth (www.mabu.dk).

Recently, I was asked to design the logo for RXTR (see Figure 2-15), a new international, modern yet elegant fashion brand. The brand image of RXTR is aspirational yet achievable, falling in line with the words *rock star,* which the acronym RXTR suggests. I created the letterforms from scratch and decided to make small cuts to the *R* in particular, which creates distinction and improves the flow by matching the same angle of the slope on the *X.*

Figure 2-15: The RXTR logo, designed by Gareth Hardy (www.downwith design.com).

## LETTERFORMS

A logo that uses a single letter or number is classed as a letterform. If a letter is used, it's usually the first letter of the brand or individual that the logo identifies. Single letterforms can be extremely iconic and powerful due to their simple structure, but they also can take on more elaborate forms. Most work well at very small sizes. Because they're simple, they're memorable. For the designer, letterforms can pose a challenge, because finding a unique solution is difficult.

The Honda logo encompasses the initial *H* drawn in a unique and identifiable style (see Figure 2-16). The iconic symbol that the single letterform creates makes it a perfect choice for car manufacturers—when it's applied to the hood of a car, it's still noticeable but doesn't overimpose. The simplicity of the iconic mark also allows the logo to be used easily on smaller areas of application such as the steering wheel or even on items as small as interior dash buttons.

Figure 2-16: The Honda logo.

Photo by Charlotte Morris

Sergey Babenko, a freelance designer from Kiev, Ukraine, designed an intricate and elegant initial for Alsona (see Figure 2-17), which reflects the high-quality luxurious private villas that Alsona provides.

Figure 2-17: The Alsona Private Villas logo, designed by Sergey Babenko.

In 2008, I designed a single letterform logo for Anastasia, an independent jewelry supplier (see Figure 2-18). The *A* initial is a representation of a diamond shining under the lights, which falls in line with the nature of the business and symbolizes that Anastasia has high-quality jewels on show.

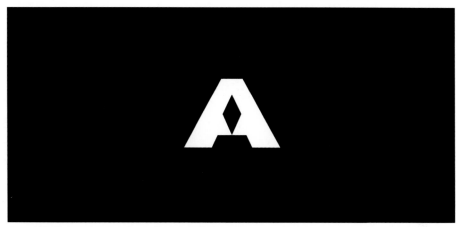

Figure 2-18: The Anastasia logo, designed by Gareth Hardy (`www.downwithdesign.com`).

## MONOGRAMS

A monogram is a combination of two or more typographic characters to form a logo. It's usually created using the initials of the individual, business, or organization that the logo identifies. The characters have to be overlapping or combined in some way for the logo to be considered a monogram; if the characters are merely placed next to each other, those are initials.

Monograms have been used for hundreds of years. They originally appeared on coins to help identify the city where they were issued. They can give a regal appearance and a sense of importance. Monograms provide a personal touch and often scale very well, providing greater versatility. Because they're so simple, it can be challenging for the designer to come up with a unique solution.

Chanel, the fashion house founded in Paris, uses a simple monogram for its logo (see Figure 2-19). Even though the brand name consists of just one word, the mark is comprised of the initial repeated twice, with the *C* reversed on the left side. This produces an iconic and interesting mark.

Figure 2-19: The Chanel monogram logo designed by Coco Chanel.

Photo by Charlotte Morris

Roy Smith, a brand identity designer from Norwich, England, worked on the new logo for Union House (see Figure 2-20), an economic development company in the United Arab Emirates. He created a monogram using the two initials of the company, which perfectly illustrates the word *union*.

**Union House**

Figure 2-20: The Union House logo, designed by Roy Smith (www.roysmithdesign.com).

Oxide Design Co., a design company in Omaha, Nebraska, created a monogram for Biatomic Point (see Figure 2-21), a rock band based in the same city. *Biatomic point* is a pseudo-scientific term for a point shared between two atoms but exclusive to neither. It's also a metaphor for an idea or feeling shared by two people—the kinds of thoughtful connections that the band hopes to make with its music. The coming together of the two initials, with the subtle electric shape in the negative space, alludes to the thinking behind the name of the brand, so a monogram was the perfect choice for the project.

Figure 2-21: The Biatomic Point logo, designed by Oxide Design Co. (www.oxidedesign.com).

# Image versus type

Designers will forever debate which is best: logos with images or logos that consist of only type. Of course, each logo project is different and the designer is the one tasked with making the right choice (if there is, indeed, one "right" option).

Here are some advantages of image-based logos:

- They help to break down boundaries and aren't dependant on language.
- They can be more applicable to smaller areas of application.
- They help to link brands as part of a subsidiary.
- They improve recognition for brand names that aren't initially memorable.

And here are some advantages of type-based logos:

- They work well for unusual and unique brand names.
- They help to reduce the extra marketing costs of trying to get the audience to understand a symbol.
- They mostly stand the test of time.
- They can provide complete distinction.

# 3

# THE KEY TO SUCCESS

WHAT TRULY MAKES a logo successful? Is it pretty colors? Fancy effects? The answer, of course, is no.

There is not one defined recipe to designing a successful logo—if there were, there wouldn't be so many unsuccessful logos out there. Still,

certain attributes contribute to the success of a logo. A logo might not contain every one of these attributes, but the more of them the logo draws upon, the more successful the logo will be.

In this chapter, I tell you what these key attributes are and give examples of logos that possess them.

## MEMORABILITY

What makes something memorable? Why do you remember some logos and not others? When you're designing a logo, trying to come up with something that sticks in the minds of the target audience, memorability can seem elusive, hard to pin down. But the good news is, memorable logos share some common traits, traits that I explore in this section.

*Remember:* Something can be memorable for good reasons or bad reasons. Obviously, you want every logo you design to be remembered only for good reasons. Anything that causes controversy or offends people will only hinder an identity and, ultimately, harm the reputation of a brand.

### SIMPLICITY

The simpler the image is, the easier it will be for the audience to remember—the brain simply has less information to process. When you think of all the well-known popular brands, you'll notice that their logos are extremely simple. When I say the name McDonald's, the first thing you probably think of is its simple, iconic Golden Arches logo, beautifully drawn with sleek curves.

Simplicity is probably the attribute that goes the furthest to improving the success of a logo. Simple ideas and imagery make effective logos.

A simple logo design improves how the logo performs at smaller sizes—a complex logo may look fine on a billboard, but on a business card or letterhead, all that detail will be lost. Plus, simple logos are recognized more quickly by viewers—they don't have to spend a lot of time looking at the logo to know what identity it represents.

Studio Ink, a creative design agency in Victoria, Australia, decided to focus on pure simplicity for the design of its own logo (see Figure 3-1). The wordmark uses simple block characters, but the small imperfections make it recognizable even when viewed at smaller sizes.

Figure 3-1: Studio Ink logo, designed by Studio Ink (www.studioink.com.au).

## THE ELEMENT OF SURPRISE

A logo doesn't have to be simple to be memorable. A logo can be memorable by showing the audience something that they aren't expecting. A logo that surprises the viewer, catches him off-guard, will have great impact and, in turn, be memorable.

Attak, a graphic design firm based in The Netherlands, designed the identity for You Can't Play a Trumpet with a Clenched Fist (see Figure 3-2). The logo acted as part of an exhibition entitled "Make Peace Not War." The loaded gun barrel replaced by the trumpet surprises the viewer and, because of that, will have a lasting impact.

Figure 3-2: The logo for You Can't Play a Trumpet with a Clenched Fist, designed by Attak (www.attakweb.com).

## TIMELESSNESS

Trends come and go in logo design, as in anything else. But you want to design logos that are timeless—that way, they won't look out of date in a year or two, and they may even last for decades. So, what makes a logo timeless? Timeless design is often simple, focusing on line work. Often, it completely ignores current or past common design trends, which makes it relevant to any time period. In a sense, it becomes pure design, which can have an everlasting effect on the minds of the viewer.

Oxide Design Co. designed the logo for Springbok (see Figure 3-3), a company that designs and manufactures precision test equipment for high-voltage power lines. The slick, precise lines make the identification of the era in which the logo was designed hard to pinpoint, and this will remain the case for years to come. The timeless illustration style allows the identity to be unsusceptible to looking outdated in the future, regardless of whether competitors choose to employ a current design trend into their own identities, thus rendering it more memorable.

Figure 3-3: The Springbok logo, designed Oxide Design Co. (www.oxidedesign.com).

## ORIGINALITY

Another key attribute of successful logos is originality. If the logo you design looks like somebody else's logo, or like a knock-off of logos that have come before, it won't succeed. But this doesn't mean that you have to start from scratch and come up with something that's never been done before. You may be able to offer a unique take on a common concept.

Kevin Burr, a graphic designer working under the name of Ocular Ink in Nashville, Tennessee, designed the logo for Ecodiva (see Figure 3-4). Ecodiva produces eco-friendly skin-care products. Nature-related imagery is overused in logos for eco-friendly organizations and causes, but Kevin created a unique twist on that for the Ecodiva logo—it's not overly obvious that the mark alludes to a leaf rather than the flowing hair of a young lady. Kevin played on themes viewers are used to associating with eco-friendly products and organizations, without hitting them over the head with it.

28

Figure 3-4: The Ecodiva logo, designed by Kevin Burr (www.ocularink.com).

I think that riskier and more adventurous designs are the most successful for any individual or organization. Of course, not every company should display an image of explicit images or make outrageous statements—this would get them noticed, but for all the wrong reasons. A logo that looks different, that makes people stop in their tracks and elicits a positive emotional response, is doing its job.

Jan Zabransky, a freelance identity design specialist based in Zlín, Czech Republic, designed an interesting wordmark for GENIUS (see Figure 3-5). GENIUS is a graphic design and strategic marketing firm specializing in brand identity, motion, and interactive design. Its focus is on building distinct and unique brands. This is brilliantly reflected in the GENIUS wordmark, which somehow manages to read well even though the word is typeset back to front with the letters upside down. Zabransky came up with an original solution for the GENIUS logo, and it succeeds, in part, because of this originality.

Figure 3-5: The GENIUS logo, designed by Jan Zabransky (www.janzabransky.cz).

## VERSATILITY

A logo needs to be versatile in order to succeed. It should allow the client room to grow, not lock the client in to one type of product (even if the client sells only one type of product at the start). And, even if your client tells you that the logo will be used only in magazine ads or won't ever be used on a billboard, a logo isn't successful unless it's versatile enough to work well in any medium.

### LEAVING ROOM FOR THE BRAND TO GROW

When companies first start out, they often sell only one product or one type of product. As they grow, they may expand into other product lines. The key is to design a logo that doesn't lock the client in, that allows the client to expand without needing a whole new brand identity.

Nadim Twal, a brand identity designer from Middlesex, England, designed the new logo for Jolly Monk, a brand of wine (see Figure 3-6). Instead of using images that we often see associated with wine producers, Nadim decided to create an abstract jolly monk character, which could be adapted and changed slightly for each variation of wine that Jolly Monk produces.

Figure 3-6: The Jolly Monk logo, designed by Nadim Twal.

## DESIGNING FOR EVERY MEDIUM

The most successful logos are those that can be applied in every medium—screen or print, large or small. There is no point in having a logo unless you can use it to its full potential.

Rudy Hurtado, a graphic designer from Toronto, Canada, took on the role of designing the logo for Toronto Star and the Performing Arts (see Figure 3-7). The identity covers all the events relating to the performing arts covered by www.thestar.com. The old-school traditional style can be applied to the rest of the brand collateral, with elements of the logo taking on more prominent roles.

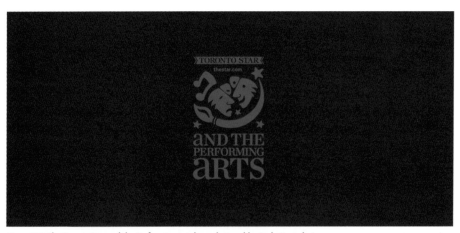

Figure 3-7: The Toronto Star and the Performing Arts logo, designed by Rudy Hurtado (www.rudyhurtado.com).

## A MESSAGE

A logo can't necessarily tell a whole brand story. That would be far too much information to encapsulate into a single image. However, it can act as the starting point to drawing viewers in and hitting them with a strong and powerful message. A powerful message that is portrayed visually in a logo design can go a long way toward achieving a recognizable understanding of what the brand stands for.

That said, the logo doesn't have to tell it *exactly* how it is. For example, if a business's unique selling point is that it sells the tastiest apples in the area, the logo doesn't have to include that selling point—in fact, it really shouldn't. Instead, the logo needs to communicate the message abstractly.

In 2009, I was approached by a startup nonprofit organization, the Information Center for the Prevention of Cruelty to Animals (ICPCA) to design its new identity. Animal cruelty is a sensitive and painful topic, so the challenge was to come up with a logo that communicated the organization's message effectively and with sensitivity. I talked with the client about the main brand message that they wanted to communicate, and we decided that the message was, "Animal cruelty has to stop now." The main goal of the organization is to make the cause known on a wider scale; we thought that the logo could play a key part in making people realize the message right away (as opposed to having to read additional literature or support-ing headlines). Instead of shying away from the sinister nature of animal cruelty, I decided to use that in order to pull at the audience's heartstrings (see Figure 3-8).

**ICPCA**

Figure 3-8: The ICPCA logo, designed by Gareth Hardy (`www.downwithdesign.com`).

Another approach is to represent the brand message subliminally within the logo. Any beliefs or ideas held by a business or organization that are illustrated in the design can help to tell the brand story, or at least form the basis for the start of communication between the viewer and the brand.

Roy Smith, a brand identity designer based in Norwich, United Kingdom, designed the new logo for the Royal Norfolk Show (see Figure 3-9), which is the largest agricultural show in the country. The show covers a range of traditional and modern events relating to agriculture. Roy represented a number of events within the design of the logo: The illustration shows a progression from an ear of corn (representing farming) to a tire tread (hinting at tractors) to birds (representing nature).

Figure 3-9: The Royal Norfolk Show logo, designed by Roy Smith (www.roysmithdesign.com).

## THE BRAND IMAGE

A logo can't do it all, but it can act as the basis for the brand identity and should help support it. The style of the logo must be congruent with the brand image as a whole to keep from communicating different messages.

Nikita Lebedev, an identity designer from Kostroma, Russia, was faced with the task of designing the new identity for an elegant jewelry designer named Muhtarov (see Figure 3-10). The intricate design of the stylized initial hints at the fact that Muhtarov pays a lot of attention to detail in its jewelry designs. The overall image created by the logo matches the brand identity that Muhtarov wants to portray to its customers.

Figure 3-10: The Muhtarov logo, designed by Nikita Lebedev.

## SCALABILITY

The ability for a logo design to remain consistently legible regardless of the size is extremely beneficial. Each logo will have a different minimum size before the identity becomes affected. Of course, the smaller that this minimum size is, the more flexible the logo.

Muamer Adilovic, a senior graphic designer from Sarajevo, Bosnia, and Herzegovina, designed the logo for a new online community named Pozzitiva (see Figure 3-11). The bird illustration is simple, composed of few paths, so it allows the mark to scale down extremely well and still be distinguishable from a standard smiling face.

Figure 3-11: The Pozzitiva logo, designed by Muamer Adilovic (www.muameradilovic.com).

## EXECUTION

You may be able to think of a memorable, original and versatile concept that you know will be a suitable solution to the brief, but if you can't execute that idea visually, the design won't succeed. The execution of an idea is more often than not crucial in connecting with the audience; otherwise they won't get it, even if you do. You can't always be around to explain what your intentions were every time the logo is seen.

Burn Creative, a graphic design and branding form in Carlisle, Pennsylvania, decided to put into practice an unusual idea for Schick Enterprises (see Figure 3-12). Schick operate a unique business that involves providing technology solutions for the pork industry. The quirky stylized mark, a flying pig drawn in an electronic style, had to have been difficult to execute in such a way that the logo is recognizable and understandable, but Burn Creative pulled it off flawlessly.

Figure 3-12: The Schick Enterprises logo, designed by Burn Creative (www.burncreative.com).

# DESIGNING A LOGO

# 4

# COMMUNICATING WITH YOUR CLIENT: THE DESIGN BRIEF

DESIGNING A LOGO is similar to tackling a maze. The designer heads down a path, possibly meeting dead ends, before reaching the final successful outcome. The goal is to keep the dead ends to a minimum. So, before you set off on the long and challenging journey of designing a logo, you should put in place a plan to make the task of solving the problem much easier.

Your role as a logo designer is to create an effective solution to a problem. You'll mainly achieve the final solution using visuals, but don't underestimate the power of oral communication. A picture may be worth a thousand words, and

that's especially true when it comes to logos, but if you and your client don't communicate well before the project begins, your concepts and ideas may end up being way off the mark.

Involving the client in your design process from the very beginning is essential, but don't forget that you're the design expert. For a designer, nothing is worse than feeling like the client is your puppet master, forcing you to use an array ugly of effects and common clichés. This chapter explains how you can avoid these problems through good, clear communication.

## THE START OF SOMETHING BEAUTIFUL: COMMUNICATING WITH POTENTIAL CLIENTS

When a potential client contacts you about a logo design project, it's a great feeling. (I still can't believe I get paid to draw!) But drawing is only the tip of the iceberg when it comes to creating a logo. In this section, I walk you through the initial steps in working with a client— from responding to that initial inquiry to setting prices to watching out for red flags.

### RESPONDING TO INITIAL INQUIRIES

Most potential clients will send you a short e-mail asking, "How much do you charge for a logo?" (Evidently, how much you charge is the most important factor.) So, how should you respond?

The best practice is not to name your rates right off the bat. First, you need to find out the specifics of the project and how much work it will entail. I always try to get clients on the phone by asking if they'd like to discuss the details so that I can give them an accurate quote. The ones who don't respond either aren't serious about wanting to hire someone or have found a designer who is willing to design the logo for next to nothing. Those who are willing to talk and share more information will see that you have their interests in mind and that you aren't in it only for the money.

When you're talking to a potential client on the phone, here are some questions you might ask to help form a quote:

- Do you have a rough idea of when you would need the logo by?
- When would you need work to begin?
- What will the logo be used for?
- Where will it be used?
- Do you have an idea of the kind of logo you're looking for?
- Is your product or service a member of a brand family?
- Is the logo for an new identity or a re-brand?
- How much concept exploration are you willing to invest in?

---

## Ideas don't come for free

If you haven't already, you'll surely encounter a potential client who wants you to send some examples of your ideas for their logo, maybe even a few sketches before they pay you "so we know for sure whether we like the logo." Never, ever give away your work for free.

You can tell the potential client that unless you have a design brief in place, it's impossible to design a suitable logo. If they buy into the notion that the design brief is important, then they should see the value in your work and respect your prices.

## SETTING YOUR PRICE

How much does a logo cost? If you plan to make a career out of graphic design, that's a question you'll be asked many times. So, is it $50 or $500,000? In short, there is no set figure. A logo costs only as much as much as the client is willing to invest in the brand identity.

Unfortunately, most clients care about only one thing when they're hiring someone to design their identity: how much it's going to cost. There will always be designers who are willing to do a job for less money. Don't worry about what other designers are charging—focus on what *you* think is a fair rate for the work involved. Clients worth working for recognize that a great logo offers competitive advantage through increased recognition and an improved connection with the target audience, and because it offers such an advantage, it's a valuable investment.

## EXPLAINING YOUR PROCESS

Most people outside the industry probably assume that graphic designers sit around all day playing with crayons and computers. In your early conversations with a potential client, explain that designing a logo entails more than picking up a pencil and drawing some pretty pictures. Talk the client through your process, outlining the different stages of development. You can even use this book's table of contents as a way of listing all the things you do—conducting preliminary research, coming up with a concept, getting your ideas on-screen, and so on. That way, the client will get an insight into exactly how much work you put into designing a logo.

39

## SHOWING YOUR WORTH

If you already have a portfolio of work, provide a potential client with case studies where your work helped to improve a client's brand identity. Real-world examples will show your potential client that your services are a worthwhile investment—one that has successful results. If you've carried out work for brands of a similar nature, talk the potential client through how you tackled the task and the reasoning for your design decisions.

## SENSING DANGER

In your initial conversations with a potential client, not only are you trying to show evidence that you're a highly skilled designer, but you're also trying to gauge whether this client is one you want to work with. You want to be on the lookout for signs that the client might be more trouble than they're worth. For example, if a potential client tells you that they've worked with a dozen different designers, and none of them provided a logo they were happy with, that's a red flag. Maybe the client just hired a dozen incompetent people—but more likely, the client is impossible to please, and you won't be any more successful than those other designers were.

Most freelancers, unless they're very successful, can't pick and choose which potential clients they want to work for—they have to take the work they can get, where they can get it. So, I'm not saying that you should be turning away work routinely. But pay attention to your gut instinct about whether you'll be able to work with a potential client. Do your homework on the potential client—both the company as a whole and the person you'll be dealing with. Use the Internet to find out as much as you can about them, especially if you're getting an uneasy feeling.

## BUILDING A REAL RELATIONSHIP

Getting to know your client on a more personal level is far more beneficial than just sending e-mails. By meeting face to face, you can gain a greater insight into the project and get to know the person you're dealing with. If the client has met you, they're more likely to trust you and respect your decisions.

## REACHING AN AGREEMENT

You may find that some potential clients won't be comfortable with reaching an agreement before meeting you first, which is entirely understandable. They may even want to finalize the design brief before a final go-ahead is sanctioned. Just make sure that you never agree to start work unless you have the basic documents in place for a designer-client relationship.

If there's one rule when it comes to carrying out design work for clients, it's to always be sure that you get them to sign a contract that clearly states the minimum requirements:

- **Billing phases**
- **Payment terms and the agreed-upon payment method** (Note: The common practice is to be given a down payment ranging from 30 percent to 50 percent before work is begun; then the remainder is paid upon delivery of the final files. Never agree for the entire payment to be made at the end of the project—that's a risk you shouldn't take.)
- **How revisions and alterations will be handled**
- **Deadlines**
- **Terms for termination, cancellation, or putting the agreement on hold**
- **Rights of ownership**

Be sure to get the client to agree to the terms that you set out for the project and make sure that both you and the client sign and date it. Don't rely on a digital version of a contract—try to get a hard copy as well.

## SEEKING PROJECT SPECIFICATIONS

After you and a new client have signed a contract, you're ready to get started. The first step is to gather some information about the project. Sit down with the client (preferably in person), and ask the following questions:

- **Why do you need a logo? Or why are you changing your logo?** This is the big one. The answer to this question should briefly cover other important factors you'll need to know such as:

- The nature of the business and what they do
- What the logo will be used for
- Where the logo will be seen

If the client's answer doesn't cover these areas, ask them directly.

- **What's the message?** I find the answer to this question to be the most helpful because it makes the client think about what they want to communicate to the target audience. They have to get to the essence of the brand—how the brand will make the target audience feel and what they want the brand to be known for. This information will also help you make decisions about the overall visual style of the logo so that it can support this message. From the client's answer, you can identify a number of key words relating to the brand image that you need to communicate to the target audience.

- **What are your long-term goals for the brand?** The client should be able to give you insight into the future of the brand, which you can keep in mind as you work on the design. For example, if the company is selling eggs right now but plans to sell chickens a few years down the road, you need this information so that your concept won't cause conflict or limit the brand. Ask them to elaborate on whom they consider to be their current competition and whom they would like to compete with in the future. That will help you with your research.

- **What makes you unique?** Clients often find this question the hardest to answer. Every business or organization has some unique quality. They don't have to be the first in their market, or even second, but at least one characteristic will set them apart from their competitors. When you've identified what makes the client unique, it may be worth exploring further, especially if these unique traits relate to their brand.

- **Who is your target audience?** Some clients will have employed the services of people who work on the marketing and brand strategy, so this information will already be available to you. With smaller companies, I advise them on who I think they should be targeting if they're not sure.

Don't be afraid to ask the client to elaborate on their answers, the more detail and information that they can provide, the better. You can never know too much about a project, but you can definitely know too little.

## GUIDING THE CLIENT

Like designers, not all clients are the same. Some clients don't reveal much detailed information about the project. Others inundate you with more information than you could possibly need. Either way, they may try to influence the outcome of the design with their own suggestions. If this happens, remain calm and consider what the client is saying—on rare occasions, clients come up with the perfect solution, so you don't want to dismiss their thoughts out of hand. If, after considering the client's suggestions, you determine that they aren't helpful, explain why you think the client's ideas won't work, and offer advice that will help to create an original logo.

41

## Taste vs. design

I find that asking the client questions about their own personal tastes in design often leads to problems. Remember that art and design are subjective. The client has hired you to design a logo for a reason—you have a better understanding of what works and what doesn't.

It doesn't matter if the client's favorite color is yellow—yellow won't necessarily be the most effective choice for the client's logo. Remind the client that you're designing for a target audience, and all your design decisions will be made with that audience in mind.

Don't be afraid to express your initial ideas, but at the same time be sensitive to the client's feelings. If they make outlandish suggestions, remain professional, explain why the idea could harm their identity, and offer an alternative. A good client will know that your expertise is invaluable and understand that they've hired you to advise them on the best possible solution for their brand's identity.

## ELEMENTS OF A CREATIVE DESIGN BRIEF

A creative design brief is a joint agreement between the designer and the client on the specifications that will lead to a successful solution. Many people think that the client provides the design brief, and the designer follows it. In a sense, the client does provide the brief, through the information that you gain from them, but the client shouldn't write the brief without your input (besides, they probably don't know how). You're the one who will be using the brief, so you need to make sure that it's written clearly and that there's no room for confusion.

In this section, I outline all the basic elements of a creative design brief. Your brief may have more information than I've listed here, but it should at least include these pieces.

The design brief itself is not a work of art. You don't need to spend hours making it look pretty—nobody will see it apart from the design team and the client, so save your creativity and time for the design of the logo.

### PROBLEM STATEMENT

The problem statement gives a brief summary of the overall task in one or two sentences.

### CLIENT PROFILE

Having met the client or at least conversed with them in detail, you should know everything you need to about their brand, but if you're working with a team, they may not all have had the same opportunity. The client profile is a short summary about the nature of the client and their history. It will help to educate anyone who uses the brief as a creative platform. Plus, it's always handy to have the client profile written down, as a reminder for yourself.

# Away from the competition

When I was working as a designer at an agency, I had a meeting with a client for whom we were designing a new identity. The client felt that we "hadn't quite hit the nail on the head yet." When I walked into the room for our meeting, I noticed that the client had a bunch of catalogues on her desk from the company's competitors. The client pointed to several of the competitors' logos and asked, "What about something like this? Or this?"

You'd be amazed by how many businesses want to look like their competitors. They mistakenly believe that companies already operating within the market have the single recipe for success. Your goal is to steer the client away from the competition so that they can stand out from the crowd.

Most clients don't trust new ideas. After all, the success of a new idea hasn't been proven yet, so clients are often apprehensive, making selling new and unique ideas seem like an impossible task. The key is to convince your client that their new business shouldn't look like every other brand in the market. Being different is the best solution that you can offer.

I've found that it doesn't matter how extraordinary the idea is, as long as it answers the brief. It would be impossible to identify a new emerging brand if they were using a logo that looks similar to ones that are already established.

## AIMS AND OBJECTIVES

The aims and objectives state the overall purpose of why the work is being carried out and how it will help the client. Be sure to include any specific requirements—for example, "to gain a wider understanding of the identity in a location or language that was previously unused." The aims and objectives help create an overall picture of the problem you're trying to solve.

## TARGET AUDIENCE

In this section, you summarize the characteristics that belong to the select demographic that the client is trying to appeal to. When targeting consumers, key demographics include the following:

- Gender
- Age range
- Geographic location
- Income bracket
- Occupation
- Social class
- Marital status

When targeting businesses or organizations, key demographics include the following:

- Industry type or sector
- Location
- Annual sales
- Size

## DELIVERABLES

This part of the brief details what the client will be expecting from you, such as the files, any style guides, or fonts (if you're buying a license for them on their behalf). Also, explain the file types that the client can expect to receive, and break it up into necessary categories such as print and screen. This will help the client know exactly what they'll be getting beyond just a pretty picture. If they require any special file types, include this information here (assuming it's an output that you can offer).

## BUDGET

This part of the design brief mentions not only how much you'll be paid as the designer, but also any additional budgetary considerations such as:

- Print costs
- Research and development (including a set fee for detailed primary research methods—see Chapter 5)
- Conceptualization (if you have a price structure in place for a certain number of concepts)
- Any other design work fees (if you're working on a complete brand identity as opposed to just the logo design)

## PROJECT TIMELINE

This part of the design brief is where you decide how much pressure you want to put on yourself by clarifying the final deadline for the project. How long it takes to create a logo depends on:

- The speed of the designer or team taking on the task
- The depth of agreed exploration
- Whether the logo is part of a broader project such as brand identity
- When the client requires the final logo source files

One thing is for certain: Creativity should not be rushed. At the same time, you can't keep the client waiting for years until you find that eureka moment that defines your career.

## A WORKING EXAMPLE

In this section, you'll find an example of a creative design brief for a fictitious company.

### PROBLEM STATEMENT

Design the new logo for a new luxurious hand-made chocolate maker named Chapman's Confectionery.

### CLIENT PROFILE

Chapman's Confectionery is a new venture started by two partners. They have been creating specialist handmade confectionery for the past six months, initially working from one of the partner's homes, but they have now secured their first official premises. They operate in East Sussex in the United Kingdom. The products they create are mainly small, highly decorated individual chocolates, but they also offer the service of custom cake-making for special events and occasions. Chapman's hopes to employ more staff in the near future and eventually convert the brand into a franchise.

### AIMS AND OBJECTIVES

The main aims and objectives of the project are as follows:

- Increase the growing reputation of the brand within the local community.
- Show that Chapman's Confectionery is of a high quality and deliciousness unrivaled in the area.
- Make the business look like a professional organization.
- Increase trust in the eyes of potential customers and clients.

### TARGET AUDIENCE

The demographics of the target audience are as follows:

- Primarily females, but both genders are potential targets.
- 16 to 65 years old.
- People located in East Sussex and the surrounding areas. (This will expand over time.)
- Brides and bridesmaids.
- People who have a slightly higher level of disposable income.

### DELIVERABLES

The client will receive the following:

- Print-ready logo artwork files: EPS and AI
- Screen-optimized logo artwork files: JPEG, GIF, PNG, and PDF

- Logo usage guidelines: PDF and hard copy
- Business-card design (double-sided) print-ready file: PDF
- Any font licenses and font files that may be used to complete the project

All files will be posted to the client on a compact disc.

## BUDGET

The budget for the new identity includes the following:

Research and development: $X
Conceptualization: $X
Fonts: $X
Total: $X

## PROJECT TIMELINE

The initial concepts are to be presented to the client by December 29, 2011.

Final approval from the client is needed by January 31, 2012.

# 5

# CONDUCTING PRELIMINARY RESEARCH

WITH THE DESIGN brief in hand it's time to embark on the logo design journey and explore your options. You can't run off into the forest of creativity just yet, though—that would be foolish. Conducting thorough research first will help to increase your chances of finding the perfect idea for the task at hand.

So, which type of research should you be carrying out? The answer to that question depends on what stage of the process you come in at and what your role is on the project. In this chapter, I focus on the research that should be carried out

just for the logo, not for marketing or brand strategy. But a good understanding of all available research methods will help your progress and versatility.

I love research, but I know many designers who find it to be a dull and boring process. Research doesn't have to involve sitting in a library for hours on end, reading up about subjects you have no interest in. This chapter details the available research tactics at your disposal and shows you how analyzing your findings can help to add focus to your creative process.

# BACKGROUND RESEARCH

Background research handles and analyzes data and information that have already been published. Background research can help you to:

- Gain a greater understanding of the target market
- Improve your own knowledge of the product or service that the brand offers
- Determine which new brands have successfully made an impact on the target audience

## RESEARCHING YOUR CLIENT'S LINE OF WORK

There's no such thing as having too much information at your disposal, especially if you're designing an identity for a product or service that you aren't familiar with. This will likely be the case, and it's one of the main reasons I find research to be so important.

You need to get to know the ins and outs of your client's line of work. Don't just rely on what the client tells you—they probably won't know everything (plus, doing so may limit your creativity). I'm not suggesting you need to learn every little detail about the subject at hand—there isn't enough time to do that, especially for smaller projects. But you can still gain a greater understanding, which will help you to think of more relevant ideas during the conceptualization process (see Chapter 6).

Going into a library and briefly reading the basic background information on an obscure occupation can be interesting, and it can inform your design. If you don't have the time or facilities to do research in a library, a wealth of information is available on the Internet. After conducting research on the nature of the client's business, if you have some unanswered questions, get back in touch with them and ask for more information.

You should be able to answer the following questions:

- What is the history of the product or service?
- What does the product or service involve?
- What production methods are used, if any?

After conducting some research on your own, feel free to go back to the client and ask if they do things a little differently from the norm (many do). It's little details like this that can help to strengthen a visual identity and achieve true distinction from competitors.

**Note:** Based on your initial contact with the client, you may already be armed with this information—it depends on the depth of your communication as you were forming the design brief (see Chapter 4).

Josh Hayes (www.hayesimage.com.au) took on the task of designing the new identity for Palliative Care Australia (PCA), which was formed in 1990 as the Australian Association for Hospice and Palliative Care, Inc. PCA works in collaboration with the Australian Government Department of Health and Ageing and the Australian & New Zealand Society of Palliative Medicine implementing the National Palliative Care Strategy.

Josh's task was not to create a logo for the organization, but to create more of a symbol/icon for a particular segment of the organization. This symbol was to be the focal point at conferences, media outings, and other public activities in conjunction with their existing logo(s). Josh talks us through his research process for the project:

*My initial research began with looking into the ways and histories of how death is dealt with, not by focusing on the morbidities of it, but the preparation, the practices, and the ceremonial activities that took place. In every culture, religion, and age that I studied, there were two common links: (1) There was always a sense of "palliative care"—some very abstract, but the sense of "preparation" was always there. A great deal of time and effort was put into making people comfortable and ready to die. (2) From a symbolic standpoint, there was a constant reference to a "vessel" that carried the soul to the next existence. In some instances, the soul was taken to Heaven (or the contextual equivalent) or the soul was given a new body (such as in the phoenix). What became apparent to me throughout my research was a core idea that nobody is alone—there are friends and family or religious officials or town/village figures, as well as gods and deities. So, that "never alone" concept became an important footnote to everything I conceptualized from that point on.*

*The idea of the "vessel" was always in the back of my mind during the conceptualization process, but I couldn't come up with an acceptable way to present it. While developing ideas, I always keep another sheet of paper just in reach, for any obscure concepts that enter my mind, during this process. In this situation, one of them was a kite.*

*Initially, I disregarded the kite as a just a random idea. Exhausted, I began recharging myself by flicking through the music channels on TV. (This isn't referenced in my sketches, but I used this in my presentation.) I came across U2 doing a live performance of the song "Kite" from their* All That You Can't Leave Behind *album.*

*It was here that I realized that the kite was the vessel and that I needed to develop it further. The kite was my interpretation of both the sense of humanity that the organization embodies as well as the symbology of the vessel idea but the symbology of end of life—this person is about to die. It's not a surrender but a fact. I visualized the kite as being the person, and family and friends holding onto the string are confident enough to be able to let the string go.*

49

Figure 5-1 shows the final design Josh came up with.

Figure 5-1: The final design for Palliative Care Australia, designed by Josh Hayes(www.hayesimage.com.au), based in part on his research into the history of palliative care.

## FOCUSING ON THE COMPETITION

Pinpointing the competitors to your client may be difficult. Sometimes, the client will tell you who *they* think they're in competition with, but their assessment may be way off the mark. Your goal in this research stage is to determine who your client's competitors are, both direct and indirect:

- **Direct competitors:** A direct competitor is any organization that offers the same product or service that your client offers, in the same target market. For example, Coca-Cola and Pepsi are direct competitors in the soft drinks market because they both produce a cola drink in the same target market.

- **Indirect competitors:** An indirect competitor is any organization that offers a product, service, or brand that's somewhat similar to what your client offers, in the same target market. Coca-Cola and Evian are indirect competitors because they're both drinks, but the products are different, and someone wanting to buy soda may or may not want to buy water.

When looking at your client's competition, you want to identify the current identities that are being used within the market, so that the new identity you design for your client sets them apart from the competition. In simple terms, you want to make your client look different from what's already out there.

When assessing the identities of competitors, don't just check out their logos. Pay attention to the colors they employ and any assisting imagery that they use. Keep a record of them if you can (for example, as a JPEG file that you can refer to later, if necessary).

Depending on the nature of your client's business, you likely won't have time to locate every direct or indirect competitor to your client. Do your best to locate the primary ones, though, and pay attention to trends you see, so that you can avoid them as you design the identity for your client.

## RESEARCHING THE MARKET LEADERS

Your client may be a small startup, aiming to compete with businesses and organizations of a similar level and size. But they shouldn't completely discount the leaders of the industry as competitors. Who's to say that your client won't be in that kind of market-leading position in the future?

The market leaders are the large well-known brands. For example, when it comes to courier services, the market leaders on a global scale are UPS and FedEx. Your client may be a local courier service operating in one city, but UPS and FedEx are still the market leaders. It's important to identify market leaders for two reasons:

- **To avoid mimicking their identities:** If the logo you create for your client reminds customers of a massive brand, your client could be seen as a cheap or counterfeit version, which results in a negative brand image and, in a way, strengthens the integrity of the market leader's identity.
- **To see what the target audience is already familiar with:** This doesn't mean that the new identity you're designing should look remotely similar to the market leaders—in fact, it should be completely different. But analyzing the logos that the target audience already recognizes can narrow your focus for exploring new and exciting avenues for the project.

## USING LOGO DATABASES

Looking at other logos can be advantageous, as long as you use it for research purposes rather than as a source of inspiration. It offers a glimpse into how companies in industries similar to your client's have tackled their own identities.

Be careful: You may find that those other logos subconsciously inspire your own concepts. This can and will happen, whether you intend for it to or not. Images can have a lasting impact on the brain, especially logos that you've been exposed to for years and years.

Millions of logos are published online and in print, not just as visual identities, but also to be showcased for research and designer recognition. Books and websites relating to logo design are helpful because, in essence, they show you what you *shouldn't* be thinking of (because it's already been done).

Part III of this book includes hundreds of logos from all types of industries that you can use for research purposes.

In addition, I recommend the following books, which include hundreds of other logos:

- *Logo,* **by Michael Evamy (Laurence King Publishers):** Showcases logos of some of the best-known brands in the world, all displayed in black-and-white so that the form of the artwork is the main focus.
- *Los Logos: Compass,* **by Robert Klanten and A. Mollard (Die Gestalten Verlag):** Has over 400 pages of logo design material, categorized by logo type for easy reference.
- *Really Good Logos Explained: Top Design Professionals Critique 500 Logos and Explain What Makes Them Work,* **by Margo Chase, Rian Hughes, Ron Miriello, and Alex W. White (Rockport Publishers):** Offers candid critiques on over 500 logos and explains what makes them successful.
- *Logology* **(Victionary):** Displays more creative logo designs that are less corporate than those shown in other logo design publications. A harder book to find, but well worth owning.

Here are some logo design showcase websites I recommend visiting:

- **LogoLounge** (www.logolounge.com): Offers a paid annual membership service that allows you to explore its enormous logo database of over 140,000 logo designs. By submitting your work to the database, your designs are eligible for consideration for the annual LogoLounge book.
- **LogoPond** (www.logopond.com): The leading free logo showcase website. With over 80,000 logos uploaded, it offers you the opportunity to research the types of logos designed for industries and markets similar to the one you're designing for.
- **Logo Faves** (www.logofaves.com): Showcases some of the best logo designs from around the world.

## Setting the scene

As I'm conducting research, I often keep track of any images that I feel may help with inspiration and improve the conceptualization stage of the design process. These images may be of anything that's relevant to the brand. You can take your own photographs or find them online. It doesn't matter where you get the image. As long as the image is helpful, add it to your arsenal. The image doesn't have to be a photograph either. It can be text, samples, or objects—anything you think would eventually help to inspire you to achieve the aims of the brief. This collection of images, objects, and other sources of inspirations can be assembled on something known as a mood board.

Make sure that you don't trace any imagery you find. Not only is that an infringement of copyright, but it's unethical and unprofessional. A mood board is meant to inspire you to create your own artwork, using your own talent and ability.

- **LogoGala** (`www.logogala.com`): Unique in the fact that the main logo featured on the site is accompanied by an interview with the designer, outlining his or her process.
- **Logo Of The Day** (`www.logooftheday.com`): Showcases a different logo every day.
- **Creattica** (`www.creattica.com/logos/latest-designs`): Has a gallery that showcases logos submitted by designers for consideration; features an array of designs for all manner of markets and industries.

## FIELD RESEARCH

Field research is collated by assessing people in their natural setting or environment, so it's particularly handy when assessing the target audience. If you have the time and resources available, field research can be extremely beneficial because it involves collecting new information rather than relying on previously published data. Unfortunately, as with trends, people's buying habits and preferences can change over time, so field research can never be 100 percent accurate. It does, however, give you a greater insight into your target audience, and it's always better than relying on your own assumptions.

Field research isn't just about the target audience. Visiting the client's place of work and seeing the brand in action can be an eye-opening experience and give you a greater familiarity with who and what you're creating an identity for. If you're working for a client who is overseas, this option probably isn't cost-effective. In that case, ask the client for as much material as they can provide about their brand. You may be able to view some promotional videos or look at pictures of their place of work. Look for anything that can give you a greater insight into who the client is and what the client is about.

### CONDUCTING FOCUS GROUPS

Focus groups are small groups of people assembled in order to gauge reactions to products, services, ideas, or advertising through discussion. Focus groups are good for gathering people's opinions, thoughts, and feelings. They're also a cost-efficient means of conducting field research (as long as you can get people to participate for free).

On the downside, getting people to participate in a focus group can be tough, especially if there is no incentive. The discussion you have can be governed by the mood of the participants, so the data you get isn't always an accurate representation of your target audience as a whole. Plus, conducting focus groups takes a lot of effort and it isn't efficient for projects with smaller budgets because assembling, analyzing, and implementing the findings takes time.

If you use a focus group as a form of research for an identity project, try to select people who fit the demographics of the target audience, so that you can gauge an average reaction or opinion to the questions that you ask. Obviously, the more participants, the more accurate the average opinion will be.

There are no set questions that you should ask during a focus group—each project is different. Try to keep the questions you ask concise and relevant to what you want to know about the habits of the target audience. You may want to discuss the market leaders, and what makes them attractive to the focus group, as well as the products and services of your client's direct competitors.

Also, keep the discussion based around the identity of the client's product or service and how the focus group would like to see it improved (if it's already available on the market). Don't ask questions related specifically to design choices, because individual taste concerning art and design is subjective and, therefore, not reliable. As the designer, you're the one who will make the design choices, based on the information you gather from talking with the focus group.

If the task is to re-brand an existing identity rather than design a new one, the client may not want to distance themselves too much from the existing logo for fear of losing brand loyalty. But if they're contacting you for a new logo, something isn't working with their current identity. By talking to target groups, you can assess how much brand loyalty is determined by the current identity, and how much freedom you have to change it. Seeking the opinion on the existing logo will help to determine why the current logo doesn't work and a possible redirection for the brand.

Consider recording your session by video and/or audio, or just by taking notes—just make sure that the participants are comfortable with whichever method you use.

## DISTRIBUTING QUESTIONNAIRES

The questionnaire is one of the oldest research tactics available. Questionnaires are great for collecting data that's relevant to your logo design project. They make comparing data much easier (because you've asked the same questions to everyone). Finally, and most important, they give you a greater insight into your target audience.

A potential drawback to questionnaires is that personal taste can affect the respondents' answers, and those personal tastes don't always apply to the whole target audience. Plus, not everyone is willing to answer a questionnaire, so you may have trouble getting the information you need.

You may think that creating a questionnaire is just a matter of writing down a bunch of questions, but you should put a great deal of thought into drafting a questionnaire before you test it out on participants. The questions you ask and how you ask them can play a big role in the answers that you receive. For example, the following question would be pretty useless:

Does a logo affect your buying behavior?

*Closed-ended questions* (those that lead to a simple yes or no answer) don't give you a great deal of insight. A better way to phrase the question would be the following:

How much does a logo affect your buying behavior?

- It is the most important factor.
- It is important but not a deciding factor.
- It is not important.
- It doesn't affect me at all.

Don't discuss existing logos on your questionnaire, because that will only lead you down the path of personal taste—it won't reflect an overall shared opinion. If you were to ask a question such as the following, you would find that the answers could be contaminated by brand loyalty and the respondents' personal preferences:

Which logo appeals to you the most?

- Mercedes-Benz
- Audi
- Ferrari
- Volkswagen

As is the case for focus groups, there are no set questions you should be asking on a question-naire—the questions will be different with each project. Try to steer clear of any questions that relate to your participants' personal design preferences.

*Remember:* The questions you ask should all be geared toward your target audience, and you should distribute the questionnaires only to people who are part of that target audience.

## ANALYZING THE RESEARCH

After you've completed your research, it's time to look at your findings and make them useful. You don't need to cover your walls in a ton of obscure diagrams and graphs, but you should identify some important elements that can help you in the conceptualization process.

The conclusions from your research findings will help you pinpoint what you can and can't do or should do for the new identity. Now that you have an in-depth understanding of the client, the target audience, and the identity that you're designing for, you can begin to make use of your research for the conceptualization. Refer back to your findings whenever possible, especially before you begin to generate new ideas.

## IDENTIFYING COMMON SOLUTIONS

Common solutions become clichés and are more often than not the first idea that pops into a designer's head when thinking of the nature of the business. Look back at your notes on your client's competitors' logos. You don't want to design a logo similar to any competitor, but identifying the common concepts currently used can help to streamline your thought process (see Chapter 6). It helps you know what to avoid, and can help to steer the client away from any persistent suggestions they have.

Common design elements can include anything from the imagery used within the logo to the colors used. If a competitor is well known for its use of a certain color, you'll want to avoid using that color for your client because it could cause confusion in the target audience.

## DETERMINING UNIQUE QUALITIES

Great logos are unique. But where does this uniqueness come from? Look back at what you found out about your client's business or organization and look for any unique qualities that could be amplified to achieve recognition. it can be anything from the unique process that they have or the history of the brand. If it can be identified as being a unique characteristic, then it could be worth exploring during conceptualization.

You may want to discuss your findings with your client to see whether they agree with your assessment and whether it's something that they want to focus on.

# 6 CONCEPTUALIZING A LOGO

WHEN YOU RECEIVE a new design brief, you may be tempted to jump straight onto the computer and start delving into the vast array of effects that creative suites offer. The problem is, creating without thinking about a suitable solution can result in logos that have less impact. Not only does a well thought-out idea save you and the client time, but the final result is much stronger, more focused, and more relevant.

When you're designing a logo for a client, your job is to provide original and interesting ideas that will appeal to the target audience. Start looking at logos in your daily life—not just those of famous companies, but the less famous ones. You can always tell when a designer has put a significant amount of thought into a logo design, and when the logo was rushed. Your goal is for every logo you design to fall into the former category.

The conceptualizing process is possibly the most vital stage of logo design. I find that going straight to the sketchpad is problematic—there's no point in drawing if you don't have a practical and relevant idea yet. So, put away your pen, pencil, or graphic tablet for the time being, and use the greatest tool available to any designer: the mind.

## UNLOCKING YOUR MIND

I've found that just like writers, designers can experience what I refer to as "creative block." Creative block can occur during any project—inspiration seems to be a distant memory, and it lasts for what feels like an eternity. This shortage of ideas can affect any designer, regardless of your skill level or experience. When faced with the daunting task of creating something new and unique, such as a logo, creative block can be challenging to overcome.

I liken finding great ideas to mining for diamonds. You'll be lucky to find one with the first dig into the surface. It's more likely that you'll find a lot of common stones before you discover that elusive gem. If you dig holes in enough places, you'll increase your chances—but it's more efficient and productive if you know where to look.

In this section, I share some of my own strategies for overcoming creative block and starting the conceptualization process.

### STARTING WITH THE BRIEF

As a designer, the brief is your road map. But it can also help open your mind and expand your creativity. Every brief contains key words that help identify the overall brand image.

Write down a few words that summarize the brief and your research (see Chapter 5), and use those words as a starting point and a guide to help you form the basis for your thinking (see Figure 6-1).

Because you've started with the key elements from the brief and your research, you know that what you come up with will be relevant to the *identifier* (the organization or individual you're designing the logo for).

Figure 6-1: Designer Oguzhan Ocalan (www.gravitart.com) shows how key attributes of the brand are linked to form the overall message.

FLUSHING OUT THE BAD IDEAS

Spend an hour or so writing down all the ideas that come to mind when you think of the aims of the brief. This will get your mind moving, and also allow you to get all the bad ideas out of the way. Still, you never know—you may be lucky and come up with a great idea during that first hour.

# Think before you sketch

Avoiding mistakes at the conceptualization stage, before your pencil even touches the paper can save you hours of time and refine your workflow. Here are some tips to ensure your ideas are winners:

◆ Avoid clichés. During your research (see Chapter 5), you probably looked at hundreds of logos of your client's competitors. Some of the logos you saw likely use similar imagery. For example, I've worked on three different identity projects for PR firms, and every single one of them suggested some kind of puzzle piece in the icon—probably because they had seen another PR firm using a puzzle piece.

Clichés are dull, overused, and uninspiring concepts that make the client's brand fade into the background. Steer clear of the mundane and try to put the spotlight on the brand you're designing for through new ideas.

◆ Ignore trends. Popular trends come and go. When you incorporate a trend into your logo design, that's like putting a sell-by date on the logo. Your logo will quickly appear stale and dated, but you want the logo to stand the test of time.

It's far more exciting to set the trend than to follow the crowd. Discovering new avenues of creativity through experimentation will not only help you as a designer but also create a unique solution for your client.

◆ Think beyond the literal. Some of the most famous logos don't include imagery of what the company does or sells. There is no cheeseburger in the McDonald's logo, no computer in the Apple logo, and no sneakers in the Nike logo. As long as the solution you come up with is memorable and relevant, it doesn't matter what the image is of. The connection between the target audience and the brand identity is the most important factor; if they remember it, the logo is a success.

◆ Resist the urge to be clever. A logo doesn't have to be "clever" to be successful. Many designers think that a logo must have some kind of hidden image that will make the viewer yelp with glee once they spot it. I've christened this "the FedEx effect." If you had any kind of formal graphic design education, you were probably shown the FedEx logo as an example of a creative and effective design. You'll have a fond memory of the first time you spotted that hidden arrow, and you may still point it out to nondesigners to show off. The FedEx logo is great because the hidden arrow doesn't intrude on the aesthetic of the design—it's simply an added bonus.

Many designers spend nearly all their time fretting over how they can include a creative use of negative space or some kind of cunning wordplay in their logos. If this kind of cleverness helps the visual presence of the brand, sure, it can be effective. But if the design ends up with a cool image in the negative space and the overall image looks like an obscure blob, the brand won't translate to the viewer. **Remember:** You aren't designing for other designers. Nondesigners won't see or think the same way that you do.

### DO SOMETHING ELSE

I find that if I spend too long thinking about a solution, it can lead to mental exhaustion and frustration. When this occurs, I put away my sketchpad, steer clear of the computer, and do something completely unrelated to design, such as a favorite hobby or even going for a walk outdoors. You'll find that doing something else allows your creative senses to rest and work subconsciously, often drawing inspiration from something you would have never thought would be relevant.

## FINDING INSPIRATION

In an interview for a professional design position, I was asked, "Where do you find your inspiration?" I later found out that I got the job because I answered, "Everywhere," whereas the other applicants had listed the work of their favorite designers.

Inspiration truly is all around. In this section, I give you some ideas of where to look.

### NATURE

We often forget that art and design are all around us—art not just in the literal sense, but in the beauty of design employed by nature. Beautiful color schemes, interesting shapes and composition . . . it's available at any time and doesn't cost a penny. To me, observing the intricate construction of a spider's web or the unique structure of a snowflake is far more inspiring than looking at a bunch of logos in a book.

## Letting inspiration find you

Personally, I find that inspiration finds me rather than the other way round. Otherwise it becomes like chasing a tire down a hill. You can't force good ideas out. Galin Kastelov, a brand identity and logo designer shares a similar view:

> Everything good is born out of nothingness. In a way, you have to stop the inner dialogue that darkens the mind. You achieve that with presence in the moment. If you don't resist the moment, the ideas will come to you. In a way, you have to stop thinking to think of something that works. If you force yourself, you get dull, commonly used results.

Panicking because you haven't yet thought of any fantastic concepts can lead to poor decision-making. Don't rush the process, but manage your time effectively. A relaxed state of mind will help the ideas flow naturally.

Andrej Matic, a graphic designer based in, Serbia, sought inspiration from the surroundings of his client while designing the new identity for the Port of Kinsale, Ireland (see Figure 6-2).

> *Kinsale is a natural harbor surrounded with beautiful green grass fields and hills. The landscape immediately came to mind when thinking of ideas for the new logo. Nature also helped me to determine my decisions for color usage—with the obvious decisions being blue for the sea, and green for the hills and fields. I wanted not only to provide a glimpse of the harbor itself but also to abstractly refer to the activities that occur there. A sail is abstractly drawn within the form, as sailing and yachting are popular activities in Kinsale.*

PORT *of* KINSALE

Figure 6-2: The final Port of Kinsale logo, designed by Andrej Matic (`www.logohype.net`).

## EVERYDAY OBJECTS

Most people are surprised when I tell them I can gain inspiration just by looking at an everyday object. But as a logo designer, you can take comfort in the fact that you don't have to go far to find inspiration.

This Is Nido, from Birmingham, England, was inspired by the pattern that a splattering of mud formed on the top of a used can of paint (see Figure 6-3).

Figure 6-3: As he was designing this logo, the splattering of mud on a can of paint inspired This Is Nido (www.thisis nido.com).

I once pitched an idea to a company called Wine Searcher, which offered online users the chance to browse through thousands of different wines online. While sitting in a bar, staring at some bottles of beer in front of me on the table, I noticed that the contours could form a pair of spectacles or binoculars (see Figure 6-4). From here, I was able to tie in the concept of searching for wines (see Figure 6-5).

Figure 6-4: Bottles.

Photo by Gareth Hardy

# Wine Searcher

Figure 6-5: The final proposed concept, designed by Gareth Hardy (www.downwithdesign.com).

## TRADITIONAL ART

Some people believe that traditional art and modern design should be distanced from one another, but I completely disagree. Visiting museums and studying the work of the masters can be an eye-opening experience, only increasing your arsenal of imagery from which inspiration can be drawn.

Denis Olenik, a graphic designer hailing from Minsk, Belarus, was asked to create the new identity for Christophor Publishing House. To reflect the brand name, it was suggested that the logo should feature a mark based on a ship captained by Christopher Columbus. Denis began researching existing paintings and depictions of the ship to gain inspiration. This allowed Denis to go on to create his own interpretation that resulted in a clean and classy image that serves the brand well (see Figure 6-6).

Figure 6-6: The final Christophor Publishing House logo, designed by Denis Olenik (www.denisolenik.com).

## MEMORIES AND EXPERIENCES

Inspiration isn't found only in objects that you can see. Real-world experiences and memories can be just as stimulating to your thought process.

Raja Sandhu, a brand identity specialist in Ontario, Canada, was faced with the problem of designing the new identity for I Can Fly, an organization that aims to arrange trips to the

United States for smart yet underprivileged young people living in China. Once in the United States, the kids are offered the chance to learn how to fly a plane and train to become a pilot.

Raja took an interesting approach to the unique task:

> *As soon as the client told me, "We're going to be taking kids in China from rice fields straight into the cockpit of an airliner—and some of these kids haven't even ridden a bike yet," I immediately realized, it's like a dream. I remembered that, as a child, I had a dream of being able to fly. I was always jumping out of trees with a trash bag around my neck in the hopes that I could take off into the sky above. I discussed the concept of re-creating this wish as it relates to the aims of the I Can Fly program. I even jokingly asked if the silhouette of the person used in the logo could be myself, as it would be surreal to see myself on the side of a Boeing 777. They took me up on my tongue-in-cheek offer—they said they'd be delighted to have me fly with them.*

Raja took a photo of himself in a flying position and used this as the basis of the concept (see Figure 6-7). The photo was traced, with the silhouette of a plane taking off as the shadow to further enhance the message (see Figure 6-8).

Figure 6-7: The original photograph of Raja Sandhu as preparation for the final file.

Photo by Raja Sandhu

Figure 6-8: The final I Can Fly logo, designed by Raja Sandhu (`www.rajasandhu.com`).

## Keeping track of ideas

When I have an idea, I try to write it down or do a quick sketch of it as soon as possible; otherwise, I'll forget it completely. You'll probably find that you can't plan ideas. If coming up with ideas were as simple as sitting down at an allotted time every day and telling yourself, "I'm going to think of some great ideas now," there would probably be more designers in the world. Unfortunately, the human mind doesn't work that way. Ideas can arrive at any time, often when you least expect them.

I keep some form of writing material and a pen or pencil with me wherever I go. This allows me to write down my ideas or even draw a rough thumbnail sketch if I feel it's easier to illustrate. Cell-phones are also handy—you can use yours to save personal notes that you can refer to later. You could even record your own voice detailing your idea, which you can save as an audio file.

Don't forget to keep a notepad and pen on your bedside table. It's common for ideas to come to fruition when you're trying to sleep, possibly because the mind is in a state where there are no distractions and you can freely wander off into your own imagination. Dreams sometimes play a major role in my work. I'm not alone in this belief—the groundbreaking surrealist artist Salvador Dalí claimed the same thing. The beauty of dreaming is that there are no rules or restrictions and, in a sense, you aren't consciously in control of your own thought process. If you've been thinking about the specifics of a project all day long, you might find that this has a direct or subtle effect on your dreams. If, like me, you wake up during the middle of the night and have a great idea, write it down as soon as possible, because you'll probably forget by morning.

Whether the ideas come to me in a bar or while I'm asleep, I stick these random pieces of paper into a solid sketchbook for ease of reference.

## SKETCHING YOUR IDEAS

There is no secret formula to sketching. Some designers find that a few sketches are enough to use as a starting point before converting the concept into a vector file. It's more likely, however, that your drawings will go through a development process, and that process is what I cover in this section.

There isn't a magical type of paper that transforms every designer's sketches into revered works of art. But I do find that working with traditional graph paper has advantages. Graph paper allows you to make precise measurements because of the consistent lines; this can make curves, in particular, much easier to draw.

Everyone has some ability to draw. Sketching and drawing, like everything else in life, takes practice. As you progress with pencil, you'll notice that the final artwork you produce on-screen improves significantly. So, don't overlook this key step.

### STARTING WITH THUMBNAILS

A common practice among designers is to start by drawing small thumbnails, which can then be refined if the concept is deemed worthy of exploration. The quality of your initial drawings isn't important, as long as you have a rough reference to the concept you have in mind.

Different designers take their own approaches to thumbnails. The general census is that thumbnails are not polished drawings but quick, small sketches that allow you to quickly see your idea and develop it later (see Figure 6-9). Your drawings can be as abstract as you want them to be, as long as they get your mind working to refine your ideas (see Figure 6-10).

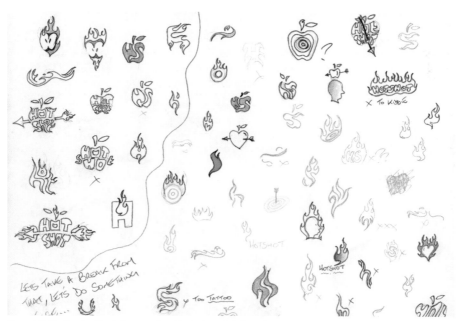

Figure 6-9: The thumbnail technique, employed by designer Josh Hayes (www.hayesimage.com.au).

Figure 6-10: Oguzhan Ocalan (www.gravitart.com) took a more abstract approach when working on the new identity for V2b.

## Be original

It would be impossible to check that your logo is completely unique—different from every logo ever designed. But there are methods you can use to prevent yourself and your client from being accused of copying someone else.

I often use resources that are marketed as being "inspiration resources" as a means to validate my own concepts, instead of using them as a starting point for new ideas. There are many logo design books that show examples, as well as hundreds if not thousands of logo inspiration websites. Checking these for concepts similar to the ones you've come up with can be time-consuming, but it might safeguard your client's new identity. Laziness at this stage could result in your having to repeat the whole process from scratch—and it might even lead to your client being sued for copyright infringement.

So, how different should your logo be from other logos in existence? There is no clear-cut answer to this question. Obviously, if the two logos are exactly the same, that's a problem—not only because you're copying someone else, but because you're failing to help your client achieve individual recognition.

A recent example of two logos that looked too close for comfort occurred in 2005, when Quark, a publishing software company, released a new logo. A small lowercase q was constructed using a circle merged with a small square on the right-hand corner. Unfortunately, Quark, based in Denver, Colorado, was unaware that the Scottish Arts Council was using an almost identical logo on the other side of the world. Because of this, Quark had to revisit the whole process and create a new identity that didn't infringe on any already existing logos.

The bottom line: Do everything you can to ensure that your logo is truly unique—or at least different enough from other existing logos that you and your client have nothing to fear.

There is no rule for how many thumbnails you should complete before you end up with a successful solution. Thumbnailing is a crucial but exciting part of the creative process because it allows you to be as expressive as you can be. It also allows you to weed out ideas that won't work. You may find that the thumbnailing process begins to inspire new ideas—seeing images can stimulate creativity (see Figure 6-11).

Figure 6-11: Thumbnail sketches for logo concepts by Von Glitschka (www.vonglitschka.com).

During my own process, I like to highlight any sketches that I feel can be taken further. I just make a small check mark next to these thumbnails so they stand out from the rest for easy reference (see Figure 6-12).

## DEVELOPING YOUR THUMBNAILS INTO SOMETHING MORE

With thumbnails completed, you can easily see exactly what you have in place as workable concepts. It's unlikely that every thumbnail will be worth exploring further, but with any luck, at least a few will be.

Now you can continue to work with traditional media to refine these sketches into something that looks more like a logo (see Figure 6-13). Experimenting through variations of the concept is also beneficial.

Figure 6-12: My own thumbnail sketches carried out for an online media and marketing agency.

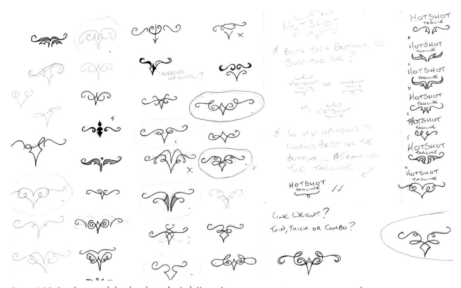

Figure 6-13: Developmental sketches drawn by Josh Hayes (www.hayesimage.com.au).

Experimentation through sketching also applies to working with hand-drawn letterforms. I was faced with the task of designing a wordmark for a homemade brand of honey distributed by Ridgeway Apiaries in the United Kingdom. I decided that the homemade delicious message could be portrayed by a typeface created by spoonfuls of the product itself (see Figure 6-14).

Figure 6-14: My own experimentation with custom-designed letterforms.

## RUNNING YOUR IDEAS BY THE CLIENT

I find it saves time to talk the client through my initial ideas instead of waiting to present everything after the final execution. This approach prevents you from putting in hours of work on the refinement and expansion of a concept, only for it to be rejected. The client will be happy that you're willing to keep them involved in the process. Just remember that you don't want them to seize the reins and begin sending sketches of their own—you're the designer, and they're the client.

After a brief discussion with the client, they'll probably give you some feedback—negative or positive. If it's the former don't just settle for one-word answers; try to get them to elaborate on what exactly they don't like about your designs. This will help you narrow the focus and improve your chances of finding a concept that answers the brief and one that the client is proud to use.

## How many ideas to present

Many designers include a number of concepts in their fee. This is perfectly fine, as long as you're comfortable with the financial reward you're receiving for the depth of exploration that you undertake. Some designers are happy that, once they've reached that set number of suitable concepts, the exploration stage is complete. I always strive to push the boundaries and not limit the number of ideas that I think of. There's always that one elusive concept waiting to be discovered. Aim for perfection—it'll be worth it.

### TESTING YOUR IDEAS

If you have the time and resources available, present your concepts to people who fit the target audience. Don't just ask one person and assume that everyone else agrees. Design is subjective. Some people have fantastic taste, and others don't—and you can't do anything about that. By collating the opinions of a number of people, you'll be able to gauge an average opinion and get a better sense of whether your idea will be successful.

Another good test is to show your initial ideas to both designers and nondesigners whom you trust. (Seeking the opinion of your friends and family is often pointless, unless you know that they won't be prejudiced in your favor.) Ask if the logo reminds them of any existing logos that they've already seen and what feelings they get from looking at the image. You may be surprised at the results.

Try to think like the target audience and forget the fact that you've designed the logo. Nobody will care who designed it—all that matters is that the idea makes a connection with the target.

It's also a good idea to test the semantics of the image. Could there be any hidden meaning or image perceived by the design you've created. View it from it from all angles and at various sizes to check that any unwanted imagery is not present.

### REFINING YOUR SKETCHES

When you're convinced that you have unique and successful solutions at the ready, try to rein in the excitement and avoid the computer just a little longer. How much time you should spend on your sketches before transferring them to screen depends on how comfortable you are with drawing using vector graphic software. You could even draw directly into the program if you find it easier than using a pencil, but I find that having real sketches is beneficial when presenting the development process at a later stage.

I carry out the majority of the drawing on paper rather than on-screen. I have fun working with traditional media—it keeps me from feeling like a slave to the monitor. Figure 6-15 shows one of my refined sketches before translating the design to vector format.

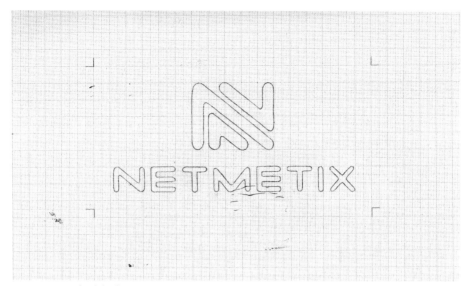

Figure 6-15: My refined sketches.

# 7

# GETTING YOUR
# IDEAS ON-SCREEN

YOU MAY START the creative process with a sketch of the logo you're designing, but a sketch is worthless to a client. Clients can't use sketches as fully functioning logos. In order for a logo to meet all the criteria in Chapter 3, you have to draw the logo using vector graphics editing software, such as Adobe Illustrator or Corel-DRAW. (It doesn't matter which program you use, as long as the software is able to produce vector-based images.)

A *vector graphic* is an image that is created using mathematically precise points joined by paths, which allows for the image to look exactly the same, regardless of its size. You can blow up a vector graphic to the size of a billboard and it won't appear jaggy or pixilated. Logos need to be functional at a variety of sizes, so it's essential that you create your logos as vector-compatible files.

In this chapter, I help you translate your original sketches from the sketchpad onto the screen.

*Note:* This chapter is written specifically for Adobe Photoshop and Adobe Illustrator, but you can use other vector graphics editing programs with similar features to achieve the same results. The key is to draw with vectors as opposed to pixels.

## PREPARING THE FILE

The hardest part of logo design is thinking of a suitable solution. The second hardest part is execution. Maybe you think your sketch could compete with the Nike Swoosh, but if you can't translate that sketch into something your client can use, it won't stand a chance.

After you've refined your sketches and given them as much detail as necessary, you need to scan them into the computer. How much detail is enough? It really depends on how comfortable you are with drawing on-screen, whether with a graphics tablet or a mouse. I'm used to drawing with a tablet, so my original sketches don't have to be super-polished for me to create the finished product in vectors.

Some designers use their sketches as guides and draw them on the computer using software like Photoshop or Illustrator, but I always find it easier to do as much as possible on the line work before the sketch goes anywhere near the computer. The line work is what's important. Don't worry about shading for the time being—focus on the paths that you'll be drawing to create the form.

If you're relatively new to drawing on-screen, get the sketch as close as possible to how you want the final logo to look before scanning it into the computer.

You'll need to scan your image at a medium resolution—200 dpi to 300 dpi is ideal. Save the file as a TIFF or JPEG. Store the file somewhere where you can easily find it, and name it something related to the project, for easy reference.

Open your sketch in Photoshop. In Figure 7-1, I'm using one of my sketches of a hummingbird as an example. You open the file in Photoshop so that you can make necessary adjustments to the pixel-based image before importing it into a vector graphic program (like Illustrator) that will form the basis of the logo artwork.

I always prefer to crop the image so that it's smaller and easier area to work with. To crop your image, follow these steps:

1. Select the Rectangular Marquee tool, and draw a square around the sketch. Leave roughly 20 pixels space around the edges.
2. Select Image → Crop. You've now removed the unnecessary blank areas of the sketch so that the focus is on the drawing of the logo itself (see Figure 7-2).

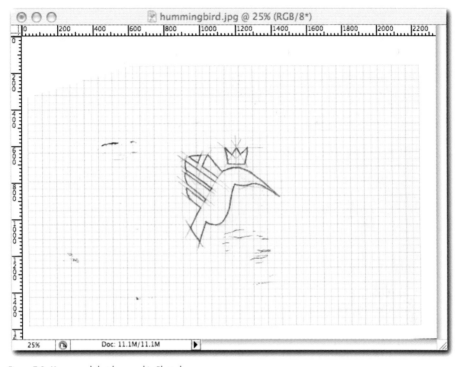

Figure 7-1: My scanned sketch opened in Photoshop.

77

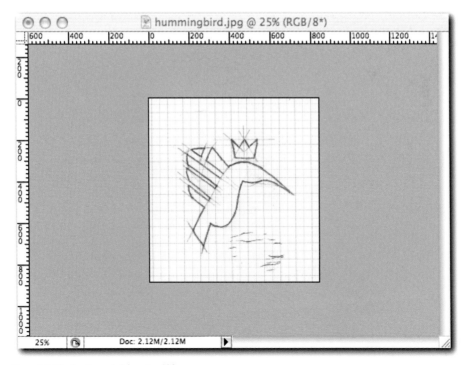

Figure 7-2: The drawing scaled down to add focus.

If you've done your sketch on graph paper, you probably want to tone down the grid lines on the newly created image so that they don't become a distraction. Here's how to do that:

1. Select Image → Adjustments → Levels. The Levels dialog box (shown in Figure 7-3) appears. You'll see a graph of data, which details the levels of darkness within the image. To reduce the level of intensity of the grid lines, you need to adjust these levels.

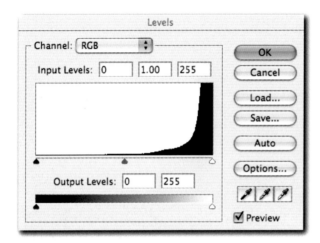

Figure 7-3: The Levels dialog box in Photoshop.

2. Underneath the histogram, there are three Levels Input sliders. Click the slider on the right and drag it toward the left, which makes the grid lines almost invisible.

3. To further enhance the intensity of the lines of the sketch itself, click the slider on the left and drag it toward the right. The sketch should now be clearer (see Figure 7-4).

4. Click OK.

## WORKING WITH VECTORS

This is the fun part, the part where you'll finally get to see your idea come to life. Open Illustrator (or whichever vector graphic program you're using), and create a new document. It doesn't matter what size the document is (you can always adjust this for output later if needed), but make sure that the color mode is set to CMYK (see Chapter 10 for more on this). Import your sketch to the work area by following these steps:

1. Choose File → Place. The Place dialog box appears.

2. Select your sketch in the location that you saved it, and click Place. Your sketch will now be imported into Illustrator.

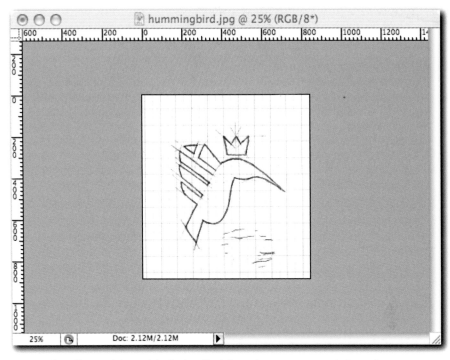

Figure 7-4: The grid lines are lighter and the sketch itself is darker, making it easier to trace the line work.

To be able to trace over the top of the sketch without causing a distraction when selecting elements, you want to place the sketch on its own layer. Here's how:

1. Choose Window → Layers. The Layers windows appears.
2. You'll notice that there is already one layer that contains your sketch. Double-click that layer to open the Layer Options dialog box.
3. Give your layer a name (I always name it "Sketch" for ease of reference), and make sure the Lock and Dim Images to 50% check boxes are selected (see Figure 7-5). Your sketch will now be on its own layer, locked so that it stays in place when you trace it, and dimmed so that your vector line work will be clearly visible.

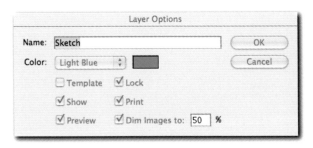

Figure 7-5: Placing the sketch on a locked and dimmed layer.

Your line work will need to be on a separate layer, placed above the sketch layer. To do this, follow these steps:

1. With the Layers window open, click the Create New Layer button. A new layer will appear above the layer that contains your sketch.
2. Double-click this new layer to open the Layer Options dialog box again.
3. Give this new layer a name such as "Line Work" for ease of reference.

Make sure that your line work layer is selected; otherwise, your artwork won't be on its own layer. To select a layer, simply click it in the Layers window. You're now ready to finally begin drawing the logo on-screen.

## USING THE PEN TOOL

The Pen tool (P) is my weapon of choice when drawing in Illustrator. I find that it offers the most control, especially when drawing curves. The places that you click on the sketch using the Pen tool are referred to as *points*. The completed line connected by a series of points is called the *path*.

Before you start drawing on-screen, make sure that the stroke color you're working with is a color that stands out against the background, I prefer to use red. This greatly improves the contrast of the line work against the background image of the sketch. Even with a red stroke, you may find that it isn't noticeable enough; if so, you can increase the stroke weight.

With red selected as the stroke color, follow these steps:

1. Find a joining point between two lines on your sketch, preferably a corner. This will be the starting point for the path that you're about to create.
2. Click the center of the join. (It doesn't have to be precise at this stage—you can alter the precision later, if necessary.)
3. Click the ending point of that line. The first part of the path is now in place (see Figure 7-6).

If your path is no longer selected, click the previous point that you created. If your drawing contains no curves, you can continue to repeat the same process you used to create the first two points. If your sketch is like my example, however, you'll need to know how to successfully negotiate a curve.

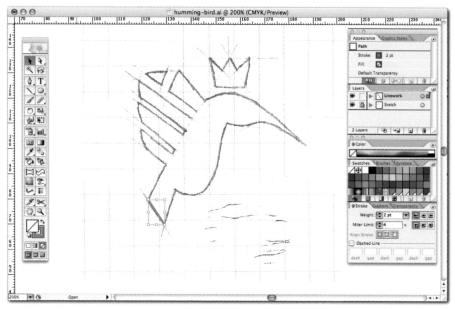

Figure 7-6: The first section of the path.

The easiest method is to draw a Bezier curve, which is created using two points. Depending on the curve, you can draw it using one Bezier curve or a sequence of many Bezier curves. (Some curved lines are impossible to draw using just two points.) The Pen tool (P) allows you to draw Bezier curves.

1. When you need to draw a curve, try to identify the middle of the curve. In my example, the middle of the curve is on the belly of the hummingbird.

2. Click this middle point to continue your path, but be sure not to release your mouse.

3. With your left mouse button still firmly pressed down, drag the cursor away from the point. You'll notice that you have control over the direction and the radius of the curve (see Figure 7-7). You probably won't get the measurements of the curve exact on the first attempt, but practice makes perfect.

4. When you have the first part of your curve in place, click the end point of the whole curve to create a new path point, and repeat Step 3 so that the curve is now fully integrated as part of the path. You may find that two points won't be enough to achieve the same line as your sketch, so you can add more points if needed (see Figure 7-8).

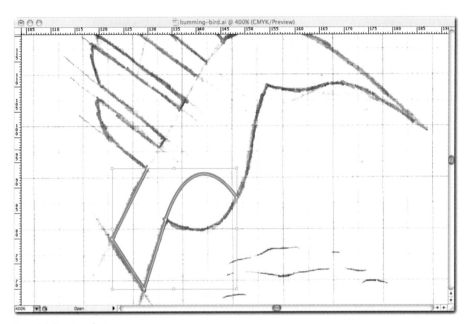

Figure 7-7: Drawing a Bezier curve.

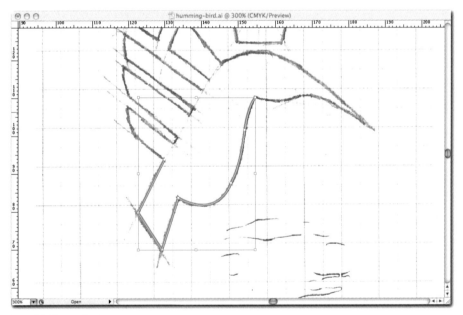

Figure 7-8: The completed curve.

You can complete the path by carefully tracing over the remaining lines of the sketch. To ensure that a path is closed, make sure that the final point you click is also the starting point (see Figure 7-9).

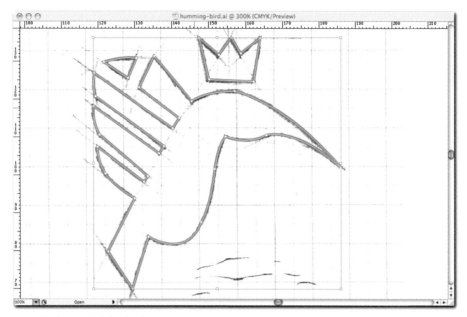

Figure 7-9: The completed closed path.

If your curves are perfectly circular, an alternative to the Bezier curve is the Ellipse tool (L). The Ellipse tool is far more accurate than drawing the curves of a circle by hand, but it works only if your curves are circular.

## ADJUSTING THE PATH

You're now done with the sketch, so you can hide the Sketch layer in the Layers window by clicking the eye icon next to it. (When you're ready to output a final file to send to your client, make sure that it doesn't include a layer that contains your original sketches, because this looks quite unprofessional).

With the line drawing completed you'll probably notice that there are some imperfections. The goal is for the path to look like a digital piece of artwork, not something hand drawn (unless hand drawn is the style of the image).

The biggest imperfection you'll notice is that the curves aren't smooth and don't flow well into one another. You can fix this with the Direct Selection tool (D). With the Direct Selection tool selected, follow these steps:

1. Click one of the points of your curve. This will reveal two handles: the point where the curve starts and the point where the curve ends (see Figure 7-10).

2. If you click one of the handles and drag the selection, the radius and position of the curve will change (see Figure 7-11). You'll need some practice to achieve the results you want. You also can edit the positions of any point on a path, again by selecting the path using the Direct Selection tool and using the arrow keys to adjust their coordinates on the document.

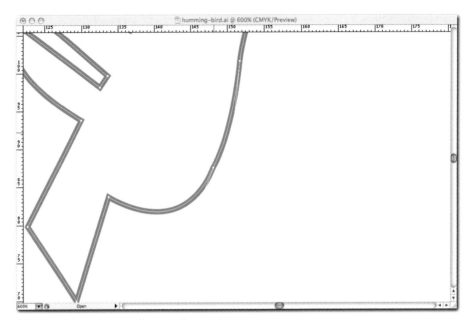

Figure 7-10: Clicking a point using the Direct Selection tool.

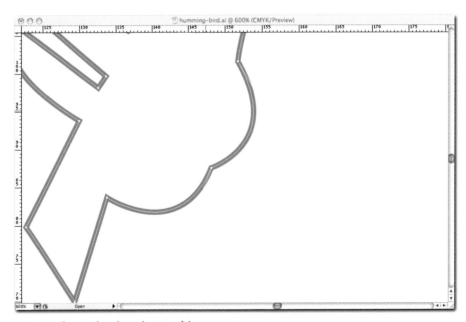

Figure 7-11: Changing the radius and position of the curve.

Another method I use to perfect curves is the Smooth tool, which is located under the Pencil tool. With your path still selected, select the Smooth tool and click and drag along the curve you want to adjust. This reduces any noticeable joins between the points. You may notice that the Smooth tool adds points to your path so that the curve is now less staggered and flows more easily (see Figure 7-12). It'll take some time and practice to get the path looking just right.

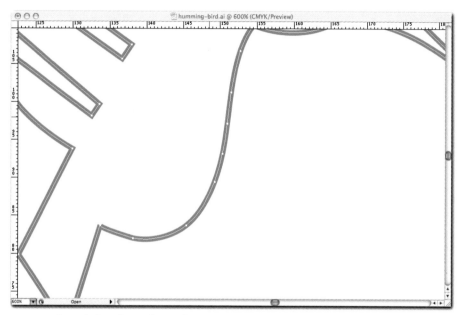

Figure 7-12: The result of a path using the Smooth tool.

When adjusting the path, continually zoom in and out to check your work. Some imperfections won't be noticeable when you're zoomed out, but you also want to get a sense for how the entire image looks.

## WORKING IN BLACK AND WHITE

With the path completed and the curves refined, it's time to analyze the form. At this stage, I always convert the stroke of the path into a black fill (see Figure 7-13). You can do this by selecting the path with the Selection tool (V) and using the shortcut Shift + X.

Working in black helps you to focus on the form and not get distracted by other design choices that you have to make further into the process. You also can spot any imperfections when the logo is scaled down or when it's reversed.

Figure 7-13: The completed path given a black fill.

To scale the image down (see Figure 7-14), follow these steps:

1. Select all the artwork using the Direct Selection tool (V).
2. Place your cursor over one of the corners of the bounding box.
3. While pressing the Shift key, carefully scale the artwork to a smaller size by dragging your cursor. Holding down the Shift key ensures that the scale remains proportional for both the horizontal and vertical measurements.

Figure 7-14: Analyzing the form scaled down.

To reverse the image (see Figure 7-15), follow these steps:

1. Select the Rectangle tool (M).
2. Draw a black-filled rectangle on your art board or wherever you've drawn your artwork.
3. Select your artwork using the Direct Selection tool (V) and give it a white fill.
4. Place the newly colored artwork onto the black rectangle.

You may want to place the black rectangle on its own locked layer so that it doesn't move as you're continually making adjustments.

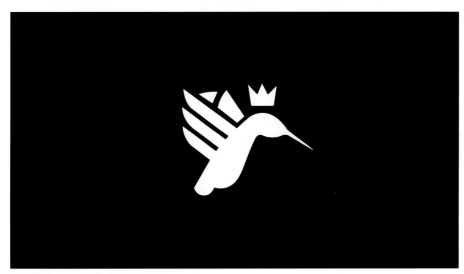

Figure 7-15: Analyzing the form reversed.

Just because you've finished drawing the logo doesn't mean you're finished with the artwork. There's always room for more creativity, refinement, and experimentation. Don't be afraid to create variations of your original idea: Remove elements, add elements, and play with the proportions and the weight of the drawing. Even the style in which you draw can be altered (see Figure 7-16). You want to carry out these experiments at this stage, before the rest of the elements have been applied—it'll save you time in the long run.

Figure 7-16: Experimenting with variations of the form.

# 8

# TURNING TO TYPOGRAPHY

TYPOGRAPHY IS THE art of creating, arranging, and modifying type. Relating to logo design, it's the way in which you visually display the letterforms or characters.

Typefaces have great influence over people's decisions, helping to further emphasize the message of a brand. The typefaces that you choose can effect whether the right message is being communicated to the viewer. Handling typography correctly is such an enormous subject that I can't explain the ins and outs of its theory and best practices within one single chapter—entire books have been written on the subject. However, this chapter does give you a greater understanding of working with fonts and adjusting typefaces to help improve a logo design.

If you're interested in delving deeper into typography, I recommend the following books:

- *Stop Stealing Sheep & Find Out How Type Works,* by Erik Spiekermann & E. M. Ginger (Adobe Press)
- *The Elements of Typographic Style,* by Robert Bringhurst (Hartley & Marks)
- *Typography Essentials: 100 Design Principles for Working with Type,* by Ina Saltz (Rockport Publishers)

*Note:* You'll frequently hear people use the terms *font* and *typeface* interchangeably, but there is a difference. A typeface is the particular design of a style of type; a font is the physical element in which the typeface is created to apply the typeface. A font is the file that you acquire and then go on to use in your work.

## Designing your own typefaces

In an ideal world, you wouldn't even use existing fonts in a logo. Fonts are available to anyone, so if you choose to use a particular font, there's no guarantee that someone on the other side of the world (or across town) won't have chosen the same font. I'm not suggesting that you should source a font that nobody else has ever used before, but over time, the more popular choices start to become more recognizable and, in turn, can make the identity that you're designing for look a little common and unoriginal.

If you can, you should draw the brand name itself as a unique piece of artwork. This will ensure that the image is completely unique, which is obviously a bonus for any logo. Not all designers have this ability—drawing letterforms from scratch is a highly specialized area. If you don't know what you're doing, you're probably better off using a font and making some modifications to it. Even then, you'll need to have a basic knowledge of drawing type to avoid making amateur mistakes.

## KNOWING WHERE TO LOOK FOR FONTS

The best and easiest place to source fonts is online. Fonts vary in their cost, but as a general rule, the more prestigious fonts (such as Helvetica or Avant Garde) are more expensive than fonts designed recently. If you must use a font for your project, I recommend the following sources.

### FONT DISTRIBUTORS OR VENDORS

Distributors or vendors are websites that source font from foundries or individual designers. They don't design their own fonts. Instead, they're more like an online catalog of fonts. Here are some of the vendors that I use regularly:

- **Fonts.com** (www.fonts.com) offers more than 150,000 font-based products.
- **FontShop** (www.fontshop.com) was the first ever reseller of fonts in digital type history, founded in 1989.
- **MyFonts** (www.myfonts.com) has a massive collection of fonts with the added feature of being able to identify a font used by uploading an image.
- **Veer** (www.veer.com) offers over 12,000 fonts from a low starting price.

### FONT FOUNDRIES

A font foundry is a website that designs typefaces and distributes them as fonts. Here are some of the best-known foundries within the typeface design industry:

- **The Font Bureau, Inc.** (www.fontbureau.com) is one of the leading designers of typefaces, specializing in fonts to be used in editorial format.
- **House Industries** (www.houseind.com), a foundry made up of a collective of extremely talented typography experts, offers a brilliant variety of typefaces.

- **International Typeface Corporation** (www.itcfonts.com) has a library of over 1,650 typeface designs.
- **Letterhead Fonts** (www.letterheadfonts.com) is a foundry specializing in fonts of a more decorative nature.
- **P22** (www.p22.com) has been providing digital fonts online since 1994.
- **Sudtipos** (www.sudtipos.com) is a creative type foundry based in Argentina, with a particular expertise in designing script typefaces.
- **(URW)++** (www.urwpp.de) is a fantastic font foundry based in Hamburg, Germany.
- **YouWorkForThem** (www.youworkforthem.com), founded in 2001, is a relatively new foundry that houses modern fonts.

## INDEPENDENT FONT DESIGNERS

You also can purchase fonts directly from designers themselves. Here are some of my favorites:

- **Doyald Young** (www.doyaldyoung.com) is one of the modern-day typographic masters. I also recommend purchasing some of Doyald's books on hand-drawn lettering, which you can find on his website.
- **Mark Simonson** (www.marksimonson.com) is a freelance type designer who has created over 30 commercial fonts.
- **Nick Shinn** (www.shinntype.com) has designed over 20 fonts that cover a vast array of typeface styles.

# Free or fee?

The Internet has opened up the world of commercial fonts to a broad audience. You have two options if you choose to use a font that you didn't create yourself: Pay for one, or download one for free. As you can probably guess, fonts that cost money are likely to be of a much higher quality than their free counterparts. It can take professional font designers months to perfect a font. To absorb some of the costs of paid fonts—and some are not cheap—you can include this cost in the estimate that you send to the client. (If you're working with a large budget, you could even hire a designer to create a custom typeface for you, but that's not as fun or rewarding as completing the task yourself.)

I'm not suggesting that every free font available online is unusable—you might stumble upon a gem in the rough. I sometimes find free fonts useful as the basis for type customizations, especially if the font carries some of the characteristics of the way I envision the final lettering looking.

Whatever you do, don't use a free font without any kind of modification. You may want to customize the letterforms or simply correct the tracking, leading, or kerning. If you just pick a font and simply type the brand name out on-screen, you'll probably see that font used elsewhere and, chances are, it'll look unprofessional without some tweaking. The biggest sin you can make as a logo designer is using an unmodified free font as a wordmark. Keep your logo design as original as you can.

## CHOOSING THE CORRECT TYPEFACE

The first typeface you choose probably won't be the perfect fit. Experimenting with a variety of typefaces is always a good thing, especially when presenting possibilities to a client.

Your typeface choices can depend on the following factors:

- The message that the client intends to communicate to the target audience
- The presence of a mark and its style
- The versatility of the typeface

### YOUR CLIENT'S MESSAGE

Every typeface style communicates a message to the viewer (see Figure 8-1). The personality of the typeface you choose should be in tune with the brand image that the client wants to convey to the target audience. For example, you wouldn't want to use a fun and juvenile typeface for the logo of a funeral director—the tone of the typeface doesn't match the message of the client. On the other hand, you wouldn't want to use a formal, old-fashioned typeface for the logo of a kids' play zone.

Some typefaces have more than one personality. For example, older typefaces may be perceived as being traditional, but in some applications they can look elegant. How a typeface is perceived also depends on the assisting graphics or brand imagery that the typeface is couple with.

### THE STYLE OF THE MARK

If the logo is type based, the designer has free reign over the attributes of the typeface. The only requirements are that the logo be legible, appeal to the audience, and be easily reproducible.

## Supporting typefaces

When you're choosing a typeface for your logo, you also want to be thinking of supporting typefaces—typefaces that the client can use for other text-based information they present (for example, in advertisements or brochures). The supporting typefaces should

- Be different enough to distinguish from the type used in the logo
- Have a similar style to the type used in the logo
- Have a style that will appeal to the target audience

Traditional    SCARY

Juvenile    Modern

CULTURAL    Personal

FUN    Artistic

FUTURISTIC    REBELIOUS

Medieval    CHEERFUL

Figure 8-1: Different typefaces send different messages to the viewer.

A logo that incorporates both a mark and typography poses a different problem to the designer. Both must have a similar (if not identical) style, so that the image of the two elements combined is one cohesive unit. Making the wrong type choice for assisting a wordmark is like dressing up in a $5,000 dollar suit only to slip on your 5-year-old sneakers before walking out the door—your image will be ruined (see Figure 8-2).

Figure 8-2: A typeface choice that has a completely different style from the mark doesn't present a cohesive look.

Try to summarize the style of the mark, and look for a typeface style that has similar attributes. Is it square? Round? Tall? Wide? By analyzing the characteristics of the form, you can narrow your choice of font from the millions that are available. The best type style choice is one that has either very similar characteristics to the mark for complete unity (see Figure 8-3) or one that has slightly similar characteristics to add a small amount of focus (see Figure 8-4).

94

Figure 8-3: A typeface that has a style very similar to that of the mark.

Figure 8-4: A typeface that has a style slightly similar to that of the mark.

## Weight

Font come in various different weights, and deciding which one to use to create the right balance with the mark can be confusing. Look at the mark again and look at the impact it has on the page. Does it utilize large areas of positive space? If it's a line drawing, what is the weight of those lines? The correct weight is one that is harmonious with the weight of the mark so that complete emphasis is neither on the mark nor on the type.

If the type choice is too heavy, the emphasis will be on the type alone, and the mark will lose impact (see Figure 8-5).

95

Figure 8-5: This typeface is too heavy for the mark.

If the type choice is too light, the emphasis will be on the mark, and the type will have less impact (see Figure 8-6).

Figure 8-6: This typeface is too light for the mark.

## Proportion

The proportion of fonts is categorized by the width of the characters and ranges from ultra-condensed to ultra-extended. In the presence of a mark, proportion has a greater significance than it does for wordmarks. As with matching the weight, it's important that the proportions of the type and the mark are similar. If the mark is wide and short, a tall and thin typeface won't be the correct choice, because the design will look unbalanced. Figures 8-7 shows a typeface that's too extended for the mark, and Figure 8-8 shows a typeface that's too condensed for the mark.

Figure 8-7: Here, the typeface is too extended for the mark.

Figure 8-8: Here, the typeface is too condensed for the mark.

## TYPEFACE VERSATILITY

There is no point in displaying a brand name for the entire world to see if the viewer can't read it. Don't be a dingbat and pick an obscure font that people will take minutes to decipher. Clarity is a must. Let the viewer do as little work as possible.

Each project brief will lead you to make different typography decisions, depending not only on the audience but also on where the logo will be used. You may be required to work with typefaces that can work at very small sizes, for example on the face of a watch. Not all typefaces have the ability to work when scaled down at such small dimensions (see Figure 8-9), so it's important that your choices have a certain amount of flexibility.

97

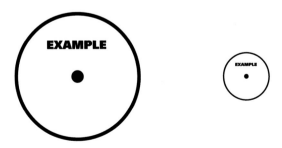

Figure 8-9: The typeface can affect scalability.

## WORKING WITH TYPE

You should never just type out a word using a font and declare it a logo—that's not professional practice. The arrangement and modification of type is an art form in itself, one that can take years to truly master.

There are many elements of typography that you must address in order for the type in your logo to look professionally crafted. These elements include tracking, kerning, and leading.

### TRACKING

Tracking is the amount of horizontal space between the characters of a font. The tracking is set by one consistent value and decides how much horizontal space the set type will take. Your decision regarding the tracking affects the legibility of the type. If the tracking is too loose, it'll take up too much room, altering the balance (see Figure 8-10). If it's too tight, the brand name will become hard to read (see Figure 8-11).

Figure 8-10: Tracking too loose in relation to the mark.

Figure 8-11: Tracking too tight regardless of the mark.

## KERNING

Kerning is the process of adjusting the horizontal spatial measurements between two characters of a font. The measurement of kerning is determined between two selected characters. At smaller sizes, we don't take notice of the amount of space between the characters of a font, because it isn't big enough to affect the legibility. However, at larger sizes, it's more apparent. Because there is no limit on the reproduction size of a logo, your kerning will come under great scrutiny.

Figure 8-12 shows the word *kerning* typed without adjustment. You'll notice that in the example on the right, the space between the characters is inconsistent. For example the space between the *r* and the *n* is tighter than the space between the *n* and the *i*.

Kerning **Kerning**

Figure 8-12: The need for kerning is more apparent when type is set in a larger size.

By making adjustments to these different values, you improve the kerning. Unfortunately, kerning isn't as easy as measuring out the same distance between each character. Some characters create more visual space than others, so you need to compensate for this. A good tip for making the kerning process easier is to flip the word upside down. This way, your eyes don't read the word, and you can fully focus on the imperfections (see Figure 8-13).

Figure 8-13: Flipping the type upside down to increase focus.

As you being to kern characters, you'll find that the space created between some character pairings can be awkward to work with. I always find *r* and *a* with tight tracking particularly tricky, because the legs on both characters point toward each other. Coupled with the slope of the *A,* this creates a vast amount of space that needs to be accounted for (see Figure 8-14). By joining the characters, the word reads more easily and isn't disconnected.

# ERA ERA

Figure 8-14: Compensating for awkward character pairings.

## LEADING

Leading is the vertical spatial measurements between lines of type (see Figure 8-15). Typically, leading is measured by a set, consistent amount when the content of the type is still editable.

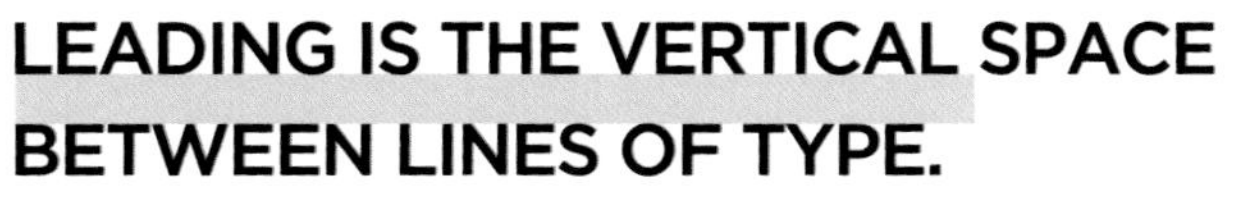

## LEADING IS THE VERTICAL SPACE BETWEEN LINES OF TYPE.

Figure 8-15: How leading is measured.

When modifying the arrangement of type that you've previously converted to outlines, you'll find that you'll have to correct the leading by hand. If more than two lines of type are used, retaining the leading as a consistent measurement ensures that the type used in the logo is easier to read as one block of text (see Figure 8-16).

INCONSISTENT LEADING CAN
AFFECT HOW THE WORDING

WILL BE GROUPED

Figure 8-16: Inconsistent leading can reduce legibility.

## USING MORE THAN ONE TYPEFACE

A logo doesn't have to use the same typeface for each word, but the typographic style should convey a similar message. If the typefaces selected have different styles, it will confuse the viewer not only by reducing the legibility but also by sending out contrasting messages (see Figure 8-17).

Figure 8-17: Typeface selections of contrasting styles can cause confusion.

Type doesn't always have to be set in the same font from a particular typeface family. Emphasis can be added or reduced depending on the attributes of the selected fonts (see Figure 8-18).

**BIG**Finance

Figure 8-18: Different weights can add or reduce emphasis.

Try to limit the number of typeface choices to a maximum of two or three. Even if the styles are similar or the fonts are from the same family, too many typefaces can make the name difficult for the viewer to decipher (see Figure 8-19). If the type isn't easy to read, it won't be easy for the viewer to remember the logo.

***Smashing*** Magazine
*Logo* **Designers**

Figure 8-19: Using too many typefaces affects the legibility.

## Dealing with large amounts of type

Having to work with what feels like the world's longest brand name can often leave you scratching your head (see the following figure). Before you make any severe changes to the way in which you intend to display the type, make sure you make your ideas clear to the client.

**Society for the Smashing Magazine Logo Designers**

An example of a long brand name.

The obvious solution is to break up the text into separate lines if the client allows this (see the following figure). The lines of type should be of similar width so that the balance is not reduced. The reduced focal area not only makes it easier to work with in the future but also improves the scalability.

**Society for the Smashing Magazine Logo Designers**

Adding a line of type to improve legibility.

If the brand name includes a signifier, such as the location or profession of the client, does it hold as much visual importance to the main name? Words such as Worldwide, Architects, and Limited don't have to be placed on the same line as the main brand name; they also can be set in a smaller size. This can actually improves how quickly the viewer can recall the brand name, while retaining all the relevant information (see the following figure).

# SMASHING MAGAZINE
## LOGO DESIGNERS

Added focus on the important part of the brand name.

## MODIFYING TYPEFACES

Altering the paths of the typeface itself should only be attempted by designers who have an in-depth knowledge of type and the art of drawing typefaces.

When resizing the typeface, always make sure that that the scale is of equal proportions. In Illustrator, press Shift + Tab while your type is selected to retain the proper proportions. If you fail to keep the proportions equal, you'll make the typeface design look squashed, because the overall vertical height or width is being adjusted (see Figure 8-20).

## Gotham   Gotham

Figure 8-20: This example shows the original typeface (on the left) next to a version that has been incorrectly rescaled (on the right).

To increase the uniqueness of the type and the design as a whole, you can make adjustments to the individual characters of the type or even the whole style, as long as it doesn't affect the legibility, balance, and emphasis. You can make alterations where you feel they could improve the visual output. For example, there are a variety of ways I can modify this letter *A* set in Gotham Medium (see Figure 8-21).

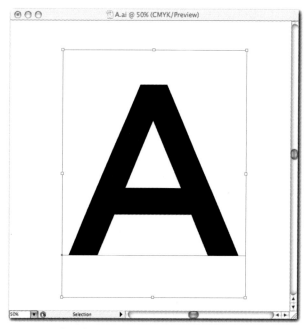

Figure 8-21: A letter that I may want to modify.

Here are the steps to take to modify a letter:

1. In Illustrator, choose Type → Convert Outlines. This transforms the letter into an editable vector path. You'll see the points that make the path (see Figure 8-22).

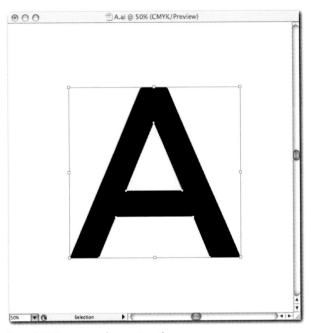

Figure 8-22: Type converted to a vector path.

2. If you want to remove any area of the fill, select the Pen tool (P) and draw the shape of the area you want to use, using a color fill of white to symbolize the negative space, while using the arrow keys to move any points of the newly drawn path into position (see Figure 8-23).

3. To make sure that the white negative space that you've drawn removes the unwanted area from the character, select both the path that you drew and the original A and open the Pathfinder tool (choose Window → Pathfinder). If you click the Subtract from Shape Area button, the white path will remove the fill behind it (see Figure 8-24). Choosing Object → Expand Appearance makes the new points editable for further refinement if needed.

There are no limits to what you can do with modifying type. If you ever adjust the height, width, or common attributes for a character, be sure to apply the same alteration to the rest of the characters; otherwise, the type will look inconsistent.

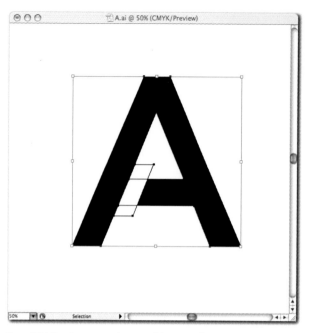

Figure 8-23: Drawing a new path on top of the type path

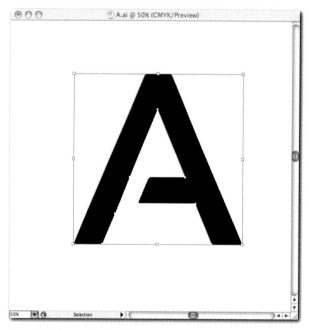

Figure 8-24: The new editable path.

## Using symbols of ownership

Some designers think that it's common practice to add a symbol to every logo they design to show that it's copyrighted. You should only use any of the symbols of ownership when relevant, not just for decoration. Copyright law is very complex, but when it comes to logos the use of these symbols is fairly simple:

◆ The Registered Trademark symbol (®) should be used only when the logo has been officially registered with a national trademark office. It's even illegal in some countries to use it without being officially registered. The ® symbol carries legal weight, meaning that a Registered Trademark has increased protection against use without prior permission.

◆ The Trademark symbol (™) and the Service Mark symbol (SM) can be used for anything that the owner considers to be a trademark or a service mark but hasn't officially registered. The ™ and SM do not carry any legal weight—they just help the client in making it publicly known that they could apply to register the logo as a trademark if they wanted to do so.

◆ The Copyright symbol (©) is irrelevant to logos because it signifies authorship rather than ownership. If the logo isn't being used by a client, then the designer may add the © symbol followed by a copyright disclaimer if it's to be shown in the public domain for portfolio purposes. You automatically own the copyright of any original works that you create as long as you can prove it.

If in use, any of the symbols should be small enough so as not to interfere with the design of the logo, but large enough to be recognizable. The common position of a symbol is in the top or bottom right-hand corners of the design so that it's the last element that the eye reads.

Is the logo really a registered trademark?

# PLAYING WITH LAYOUT

HERE'S A QUESTION for you: What's the best way to arrange a deck of playing cards? Would you opt for the easy way of just placing them flat on the table, or would you be more adventurous and arrange them to create an impressive house of cards? The best way depends on your goal— what you plan to do with that deck of cards. The same principle applies when deciding on the layout for a logo design. The truth: There isn't a best way at all.

This chapter explores how working with layout doesn't have to be boring and predictable. As with every other design element, layout gives you the opportunity to be creative.

# WORKING WITH ALIGNMENT

Alignment concerns the placement of the elements in relation to one another. Many logo designers either rush through this part of the process or overlook it completely. But alignment plays an important role in a logo and shouldn't be ignored.

Your alignment choice will be based on a number of factors:

- **The form of the elements:** The shape of a mark can dictate the alignment of assisting type in order to achieve balance.
- **Where the logo will primarily be applied:** If the dimension of the application has either a dominant horizontal or vertical measurement, you'll want to test whether your design will make the best use of the space available. You may find that you have to offer more than one alignment option for different applications.
- **Most important, the subjective opinion of the designer:** There are no rules set in stone, so your own judgment will be the deciding factor when it comes to alignment. Continually guide the client toward the alignment you think works best.

## LOOKING AT COMMON ALIGNMENT OPTIONS

If you have a mark with assisting type, you could just lump the two together and hope for the best, but that probably won't help to achieve the maximum impact and unity between the two separate elements. You can pretty much display the two elements in any alignment you want, as long as they look connected. If you place the mark too far away from the type, this could appear disjointed and could even come across as two separate logos.

In this section, I show you some common options, as well as explore more creative and unusual decisions.

### Stacked

Probably the easiest way to align your logo is it to stack the mark and type on top of each other (see Figure 9-1). Take a look at many of the world's most famous logo designs, and you'll see stacked alignment. However, stacked alignment isn't always best. In Figure 9-1, there isn't a complete unification between the mark and the type.

Figure 9-1: Stacked alignment.

## Horizontal

Horizontal alignment is placing the type and mark directly adjacent to each other. You can arrange the logo so that the mark is on the left (see Figure 9-2) or on the right (see Figure 9-3). The viewer will likely notice whatever's on the left first, because we're used to reading from left to right, so keep this in mind as you decide which arrangement you prefer. (Of course, in some languages the viewer reads from right to left, so keep this in mind if your client and the target audience are located in an area where this is the case.)

Figure 9-2: Horizontal alignment with the mark on the left.

Figure 9-3: Horizontal alignment with the mark on the right.

The form of the mark also can play an important role in where the eye is drawn. In my example, you'll notice that, on the right of the mark, the beak of the hummingbird is narrow and pointed, which forces the eye to the right. If this mark is placed to the left of the type, it leads the eye to read the type, but if the mark is placed to the right of the text, it points toward white space.

## EXPERIMENTING

Don't think that the only way to align objects is to place them directly adjacent to each other or stacked high; there are many alignment options beyond the most common ones. If the alignment of your logo looks a little different from the norm, it may help increase recognition, as long as the logo isn't one big jumbled mess that the viewer can't begin to comprehend.

Be creative with your alignment choices and explore the endless possibilities (see Figure 9-4). Even then, if you do come up with a more adventurous and unusual layout, you may have to convince the client it will work.

## DEALING WITH AWKWARD SHAPES

Some shapes have a way of giving designers headaches. The goal is a harmonious balance between a mark and the type, but some shapes make this more challenging than others. Circular and square shapes are typically quite easy to balance, but shapes that have no defined classification can be a little trickier.

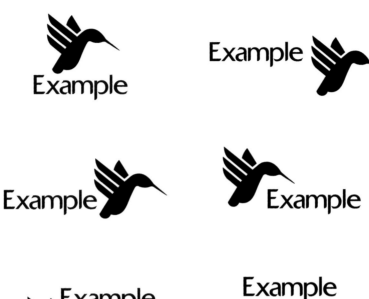

Figure 9-4: Experimenting with alignment.

For example, if the shape of the mark forms a perfect triangle, but the overall shape of the typography is more rounded, it will clash. The selection of typography should help, but some marks can be tricky to align regardless of the type. In my example, the mark doesn't fill a defined area—it's wider in some places than others, mainly because of the narrow space that the hummingbird's bill forms (see Figure 9-5). There is a greater amount of negative (or white) space in the bottom-right area. As a result, if the mark were to be placed directly above the assisting type, I'd have to counter this so that the focus isn't placed on that awkward area.

Figure 9-5: Identifying the positive and negative space of a mark.

In my choice for alignment, I chose to place the mark at a diagonal angle to the type, so that it fills part of the negative space (see Figure 9-6). This also makes it look more natural, as if the hummingbird is hovering above the type, but it still faces toward the right, forcing the eye to read the brand name.

116

Figure 9-6: Making allowances for the negative space that awkward shapes can create.

## CREATING THE RIGHT BALANCE

Another key aspect of layout is balance. You want the proportion of each element in the logo—the mark and the text—to result in a design that's balanced, where neither element overpowers the other. You also can use the rule of thirds to refine the logo's balance.

## PROPORTION

When it comes to proportion, there are no hard-and-fast rules—as long as the type and the mark are legible, you can experiment until you achieve the right balance. ***Remember:*** Especially for new brands, the type is critical—it communicates the name of the brand and must be easy to read.

Proportion also may depend on the nature of the mark. In my example, the mark is a literal pictorial illustration of a hummingbird, so if I were to scale it in a gigantic size compared to the type, it would start to look unnatural (unless there is a rare breed of gigantic hummingbird that I'm not aware of). On the other hand, I don't want the mark to be so small that it becomes unnoticeable.

As with the alignment, the best way to achieve balance between two or more elements is to experiment with as many options as possible. I played with the proportion in my example to see what works best (see Figure 9-7).

Figure 9-7: Experimenting with proportion.

## THE RULE OF THIRDS

If you want to be more precise than using the naked eye to create balance, you can apply the rule of thirds, which has been used in art and design for hundreds of years (initially as a means of proportioning scenic paintings). The rule of thirds divides an image into nine equal parts, to create a 3 x 3 grid.

In my example, I've placed my chosen layout for the logo in a rule-of-thirds grid (see Figure 9-8). You'll notice that, even though the mark slightly overlaps the area of the typography, the ratio is roughly 1:2 in favor of the type by horizontal measurement. By the vertical measurement, the ratio is roughly 2:1 in favor of the mark. This is what works in my example because of the unusual shape of the mark. For other logos, it may be the other way around.

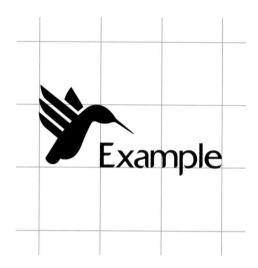

Figure 9-8: Applying the rule of thirds.

In Figure 9-9, you can see my final chosen layout with the proportion and rule of thirds applied.

The rule of thirds can help you achieve balance in your logo, but rules are made to be broken. Don't be a slave to the rule of thirds. Use it as a tool—one of many tools, including your own personal preference, in your arsenal.

Figure 9-9: The final layout.

# 10 CONSIDERING COLOR

COLOR PLAYS AN integral part in the recognition of brands. Think of Pepsi and Coke, for example—two massive competitors in the soft-drinks market. One uses blue; the other, red. This significant difference helps the consumer distinguish between the two. If both used the same color, consumers would have a much harder time identifying the one they were looking for on the shelves of their local supermarket—they'd have to look even harder at the packaging. The fact that you can tell the difference between bottles of Coke and bottles of Pepsi from a distance, even without being able to identify the logo, shows just how important color is to brand identity.

In this chapter, I explain how to make the best color choices and ensure that the colors you choose remain consistent across all media.

## THE PSYCHOLOGY OF COLOR

Research has shown that color has a direct effect on our behavior and moods. Color can alter the choices we make and the products we buy. An effective brand color or palette is one that effectively supports the brand image while making a connection with the target audience.

### BLACK

Black is the most powerful color in the spectrum. It exudes luxury but also can symbolize death and misery. Guinness, brewer of the popular Irish stout, uses black as its main brand color to reflect the color of the product.

### WHITE

White signifies cleanliness and purity, explaining why it's the uniform color of doctors and nurses. White also is used heavily in interior design—it's a neutral and light color that can make small areas look larger than they are due to the amount of light that it reflects. White also is seen as a color of luxury. Apple uses white in the design of its products and packaging to create a stylish and luxurious brand image.

### RED

Red is the color that affects people the most—it intensifies our emotions on many different levels, at both ends of the spectrum. It's the color of love and romance, as well as anger (think of people getting red in the face with rage).

## ORANGE

Orange is the most exciting color in the spectrum. It radiates warmth and energy. Orange is strongly associated with positivity and a new dawn, which is why the telecommunications company of the same name use the color for its brand name, color, and slogan ("The future's bright, the future's orange").

## YELLOW

Yellow is the hardest color for the human eye to process because of its intensely bright hue. Yellow should be used sparingly, not over vast areas. When used in context, yellow can be a cheerful and happy color, perhaps because of its connection to the color of the sun. McDonald's take advantage of this relationship by using the color yellow for its Golden Arches.

## GREEN

Green is the most dominant color in nature. It's relaxing and reassuring, making it the perfect choice for businesses claiming to be eco-friendly. You'll notice that green is used on the packaging of healthy foods, to try to influence consumers' shopping habits. Subway is one multinational company using green to great effect; by using green on its storefronts, menus, and packaging, Subway has played a major role in convincing consumers that it's the healthy fast-food alternative to McDonald's and KFC.

Have you ever heard your favorite late-night talk-show host refer to celebrities waiting in the "green room"? Those rooms have been painted green to try to calm guests' nerves before walking out onstage.

123

### BLUE

Blue is the most common corporate color because it's viewed as the least threatening and most trusting color. This explains why large financial institutions such as Barclaycard use blue as their main brand color. Ford uses it to help convince potential buyers that its cars are reliable, which is even more important when the product is expensive.

### PURPLE

Purple is traditionally associated with royalty and luxury. It's said to help increase our creativity. One company that famously uses the color purple is Cadbury, the confectionary company based in Birmingham, England. Cadbury uses the color purple to create a luxurious perception of the chocolate it sells. Cadbury has even copyrighted the use of the Pantone 2685C or "Cadbury Purple," as it's commonly known, to help protect the brand's identity.

### BROWN

Brown signifies the earth, the outdoors, and comfort. It also can be linked with reliability, which could be why UPS uses brown in its logo, on its trucks, in employee uniforms, and on its packaging. Brown also can be seen as dull and boring due to its lifeless pigment.

## CHOOSING A PALETTE

The colors you choose may be affected by many factors, including the following:

- **The characteristics of the target audience:** You don't have to adhere to traditional stereotypical tastes, but keep in mind that some colors won't be appealing to some audiences. For example, bright colors aren't suitable for the identity of a funeral parlor because they conflict with the sensitive brand image.
- **Any specifications in the brief relating to colors to be used or avoided:** Your client may be adamant that they definitely do or do not want to use a certain color or colors.
- **The colors used by the client's competitors:** In some markets, a brand can be so powerful that a color is often directly associated with a brand name, so using the same color would not be ideal to achieve true distinction.
- **Where the logo will be used:** In some cases, the environment and surroundings of where the logo will be applied or viewed could restrict or dictate the colors that can be used.

The color wheel (see Figure 10-1) helps explain the relationships between the different hues. When you're choosing a color palette, the color wheel will make your life a lot easier.

125

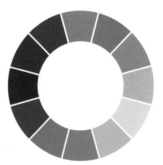

Figure 10-1: The color wheel shows the relationship between hues in the spectrum.

You may be wondering why white and black aren't on the color wheel. Technically, white and black aren't colors—white is the absence of color and black is the darkest shade, regardless of the hue. As neutrals, white and black are harmonious with any color.

As an example of applying color to a logo, I'll use Figure 10-2. For increased impact, I'll apply a different hue to the mark than I apply to the background. The background doesn't need to have a color. You should always test whether the colors that you use will work on white and, if necessary, on black. Try to think of situations where a background color will be applied and how the color of the logo will work.

Figure 10-2: A sample logo.

## COMPLEMENTARY

Selecting hues from the opposite sides of the color wheel creates a complementary color scheme (see Figure 10-3).

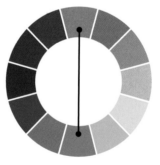

Figure 10-3: A complementary color scheme.

## How many colors?

Designers often debate the number of colors that should be used in a logo. Years ago, the use of more than three colors in a logo was extremely expensive to reproduce in print. Luckily, print technology has improved a great deal in the last decade or more, allow designers more freedom than they previously had. But, even though technology has advanced, the more colors you use, the more expensive it will be—especially if you're printing solely using Pantone colors.

Because they're on opposite sides of the color wheel, complementary colors are those that have the highest contrast between one another, creating an increased level of vibrancy (see Figure 10-4).

Figure 10-4: A complementary color scheme in use. The blue shade is opposite the tan color on the color wheel.

### MONOCHROMATIC

Selecting one hue as the basis for a scheme, with varied intensities and shades of that hue, is a monochromatic palette (see Figure 10-5).

Monochromatic schemes are easy on the eye because of the lack of contrast, but if they aren't handled correctly, they can look flat and have a reduced impact (see Figure 10-6).

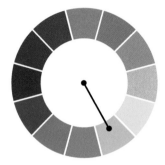

Figure 10-5: A monochromatic color scheme.

Figure 10-6: A monochromatic color scheme in use. The palette is created by shades of the green hue.

## TRIADIC

A triadic color scheme, as the name suggests, is composed of three equally spaced main colors. If you were to draw a line between each selection on the color wheel, it would form a triangle (see Figure 10-7).

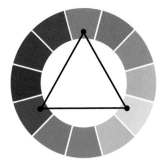

Figure 10-7: A triadic color scheme.

Similar to a complementary scheme, colors selected in a triadic palette have high levels of contrast, but the addition of a third hue increases the balance (see Figure 10-8). Triadic color schemes don't work so well if all the hues are of a high level of saturation.

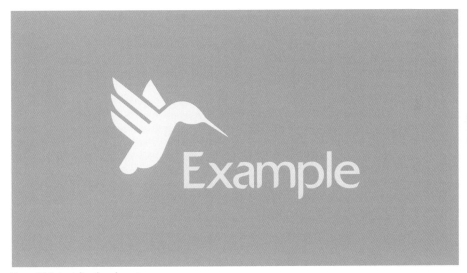

Figure 10-8: A triadic color scheme in use.

## ANALOGOUS

Colors directly next to each other on the color wheel form an analogous palette (see Figure 10-9).

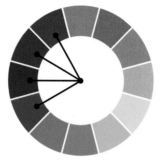

Figure 10-9: An analogous color scheme.

Because the colors in an analogous palette are adjacent to one another on the color wheel, there is reduced contrast, which increases the harmony (see Figure 10-10).

Figure 10-10: An analogous color scheme in use.

# Color palette resources

Luckily, there are some websites that can make picking color schemes an easier process for you if you don't yet feel comfortable using your own judgment. I recommend the following resources for creating and browsing color palettes for use in your work:

- Kuler (`http://kuler.adobe.com`) allows you to choose palettes based on type or create your own using custom values.
- COLOURlovers (`www.colourlovers.com`) is a website dedicated to the creation of palettes. It showcases palettes created by community members.
- Color Scheme Designer (`www.colorschemedesigner.com`) is focused on the color wheel to choose your colors, with a maximum of four colors within a scheme.

## RGB VS. CMYK, SCREEN VS. PRINT

You can never guarantee that a logo will be used for only one specific medium, whether that's screen or print. Even organizations that operate solely online will, at some point, have to send out collateral that features their logo. Unfortunately, the biggest headache for designers is when a color is not output using the same method on-screen or in print. Screen and print use different color models.

The colors you see on-screen are formulated by the colors red, green, and blue (RGB). To make things even more confusing, there are different methods of using inks in print. The most common is the four-color process that is composed of cyan, magenta, yellow, and black (CMYK).

Figure 10-11 shows how both the RGB color models are created. Colors that you're able to see are created by the presence of light. Turn off your monitor, and you'll notice that the screen is black, because the monitor is not emitting any light. The presence of light forms the colors, which means that RGB is *additive*. In print, the colors are created via light that is reflected rather than emitted. By printing inks onto a material, it masks the reflection of light caused by the original color of the material (which isn't always white). The absence of ink will be the color of the material—thus, CMYK is *subtractive*.

CMYK is effective, but you can never guarantee that each printer will use the same values of cyan, magenta, yellow, and black inks to achieve the exact same output. An alternative is to use Pantone colors, which offer a greater level of consistency, because they're preformulated inks that are used by printers internationally.

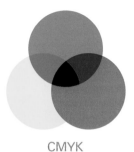

RGB          CMYK

Figure 10-11: How the RGB and CMYK color modes are achieved.

One of the most valuable investments that a designer can make is the purchase of a Pantone Color Book (available from www.pantone.com). The swatch book shows the true representation for how the colors will print when using Pantone inks. The different swatch formula guides can even show which color to select depending on the finish of the material you're printing on. It will tell you whether the Pantone ink is achievable in both CMYK and RGB, which can save you time.

Your vector-based software can display a vast selection of different color swatch libraries, both in CMYK and in RGB. Some colors in RGB won't be achievable in CMYK, so you need to check that your choice is achievable in both. If you don't have a Pantone Color Book, you can do this by selecting a color in RGB color mode and changing to CMYK color mode. If a change occurs (which it most likely will), then you'll have to make some slight adjustments so that the difference in color is not as noticeable. Using the Pantone Matching System (PMS) via the Pantone Color Book is the most accurate and easiest way to check the output and versatility of your color choices.

I find it easiest to start in the CMYK color mode and work backward, because I know that when the document is converted to RGB there will be less of a difference. Also, if you already have the value for an achievable color in CMYK, you can easily obtain the RGB values and web hex code by double-clicking on the swatch in Adobe Illustrator. Most designers start with Pantones and then find the CMYK values, followed by RGB.

A designer can never learn enough about printing methods. If you're lucky enough to be offered a tour around a printing press, take it—it can only increase your level of understanding.

## Calibrating your monitor

Have you ever noticed that when you view your work on two different monitors, the colors don't always look the same? This is due to a difference in the way the colors settings have been calibrated. Calibration of your monitor is important so that you can view the true intensity of the hues that you're working with.

Mac OS X has a built-in option of calibrating your monitor through System Preferences → Displays → Color → Calibrate. But I prefer to use a special device called a Pantone huey that attaches externally to the monitor and does the calibration for me.

Be prepared for the colors that you choose to look different on other monitors—usually, the client's. When dealing with color, I always try to explain to the client the basic differences that can occur, both on-screen and in print, so that there are no surprises when they receive the final artwork. (This is also another reason why it's a good idea to get print proofs so that the client can see exactly how the colors will look.) You may even want to explain to your clients the importance of calibrating their monitors, so that they're seeing the same thing you're seeing.

# 11 PRESENTING YOUR DESIGNS TO YOUR CLIENT

SELLING YOUR IDEAS and creativity is a tough business. Presentation is the downfall of many talented designers. Great designers, especially freelancers, have to play many different roles—it's not enough to have fantastic design skills if you want to have a successful career. The good news is, if you've been working all along to build a strong relationship with your client through effective communication at the earliest stages of forming the brief, you won't have a problem in getting your clients to trust you and your creativity.

In this chapter, I walk you through the presentation process, from preparing, to selling your idea, to handling client feedback, to revising your designs based on that feedback.

## PREPARING TO TAKE THE STAGE

With your concepts at the ready, it's time to convince the client that your solutions will help their brand. *Remember:* Your presentation of your ideas decides the future of your concept. You don't want to spend hours or weeks on the development and exploration of a concept only to fail to show it to the client in the best possible way.

After you've given your presentation, your clients may ask questions. Try to anticipate what those questions might be, and make notes on how you want to respond, as well as any factors that could help to sell your idea.

### CHOOSING YOUR MEDIUM

The first step to preparing for your presentation is deciding on the best method for delivering your concepts. The answer really depends on the environment in which you'll be making your presentation and what you feel most comfortable with. If you live in the same area as your client, try to arrange a face-to-face meeting. Speaking before an audience is often nerve-wracking, but meeting face-to-face allows you to gauge their reactions more easily than you can over the phone or Internet.

You can reduce some of your nervousness by practicing your presentation in front of family, friends, or colleagues beforehand. This will also help you identify anything you need to change in the presentation.

If I'm dealing with a client who is based overseas, I often create a presentation area on my own website, especially for that client (see Figure 11-1). I create a page for each concept separately, because I find that showing all the concepts at the same time can be a bit too much information to take in. After my concepts have been uploaded online, I arrange a suitable time to speak with the client on the phone and talk them through each concept. Your client may also be willing to talk via video chat, through a service like Skype (www.skype.com); video chat isn't quite as good as face-to-face communication, but it does at least allow you to see their facial expressions.

*Never* send clients vector graphics of your concepts—the client could be able to start using the logo before they've even paid for it. I suggest sending JPEGs as standalone images or embedded in a locked PDF document if possible. This helps to protect your work before the final signoff (and before you've been paid).

Figure 11-1: An example of an online presentation for a client.

## Letting your designs breathe

Ever heard of the phrase "stand back and admire your work"? If you view an object up close, you can't see it in all its glory. Placing logo concepts in a file and scaling them so that the fit the whole of the available area reduces the focus (see the first figure).

Providing sufficient space around the edges of the artwork allows the design to breathe (see the second figure). I always aim for the logo to take up roughly 50 percent of the surface area of the medium in which it will be presented.

continued

continued

Poor presentation of a logo.

Strong presentation of a logo.

## KNOWING HOW MUCH TO SHOW

Going into a presentation with only one concept is a tremendous risk—one you don't want to take. If the client doesn't like it, you've got nothing. Instead, you want to present a variety of concepts.

Choice is always a good thing, especially when dealing with identity. Offering concepts that are too similar makes the project claustrophobic. Thorough exploration and development along various avenues will allow you to pinpoint different types of solutions. Figure 11-2 shows three different concepts I presented for one project, all answering the design brief.

139

Figure 11-2: Three concepts I designed, all answering the same design brief.

Von Glitschka presented six different logo concepts to his client Hepburn Creative to show that he had thoroughly explored the options (see Figure 11-3).

Figure 11-3: Six concepts designed by Von Glitschka (www.vonglitschka.com).

This isn't about providing a couple of rushed, poorly formed concepts alongside one concept that you think is the winner. Chances are, the client will pick the concept you didn't put much thought into, and you won't be happy. Make sure that all the concepts you present are of the same high standard—that way, you'll be happy that you've delivered your best service no matter what the client chooses. **Remember:** Not just the client's reputation is at stake—your own reputation is on the line, too.

## SHARING YOUR VISION

Clients aren't mind-readers. You may be able to reel off a ten-minute speech about how awesome the logo will look when it's letter pressed into the finest paper ever produced, but your spiel will mean nothing to the client unless they can see it for themselves.

You can help the client imagine how the logo will be used and expanded by creating mockups of anything you feel it could be applied to. (As a bonus, these mockups could even lead to future work on the brand collateral if you've been contracted only to design the logo.)

Jan Zabransky, a freelance graphic designer from the Czech Republic who specializes in logo and identity design, was asked to create the logo for a new cafe called Coffee Cup. Having decided on an interesting concept (see Figure 11-4), he showed the client how that concept could be used in application (see Figure 11-5). In the file sent to the client by Jan, he demonstrated how the logo could be used and would look on items that he felt relevant to the nature of the client. In this case, on coffee cups, menus and packaging. The file also displays the type of assisting graphics (the dark texture) can help to enforce the brand image.

Figure 11-4: The Coffee Cup concept, design by Jan Zabransky (www.janzabransky.cz).

141

Help the client to realize how much branding potential there is for the concept by applying it to any media that you think will use the logo. In Figure 11-6, designer Von Glitschka shows how elements of the Hepburn Creative logo (refer to Figure 11-3) can be extended to the rest of the brand collateral.

Figure 11-5: An application mockup for Coffee Cup, created by Jan Zabransky using Photoshop.

143

Figure 11-6: Elements of the Hepburn Creative logo can be extended to the brand collateral, and designer Von Glitschka (www.vonglitschka.com) shows his clients how in this presentation.

In Figure 11-7, designer Oguzhan Ocalan lets the client imagine what the logo will look like in their hands.

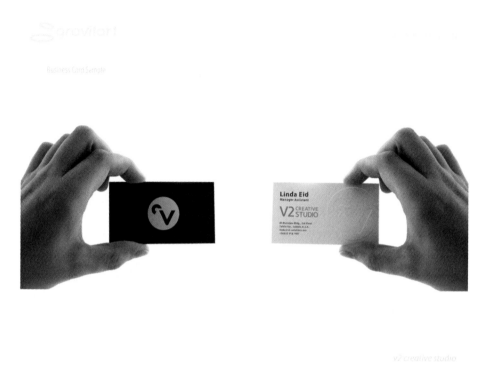

Figure 11-7: Oguzhan Ocalan (www.gravitart.com) lets the client imagine what the logo will look like in their hands.

Finally, in Figure 11-8, designer Nadim Twal takes the presentation process one step further by creating 3D renderings of the product and applying the logo to them, so that the client can see how well the concept performs.

Figure 11-8: Nadim Twal's presentation of the Carakale logo allows the client to visualize the logo in action on the product that it represents.

145

## SELLING YOUR IDEAS

After you've prepared for your presentation (see the previous section), you've done most of the work. Now you just have to sell your ideas to the client. Notice that I said "sell your ideas," not "run your ideas by." E-mailing your logo concepts to the client, crossing your fingers, and hoping for a positive outcome won't get you very far. You need to talk to your client about your concepts and help your client imagine using them.

You can't just say to the client, "I think we should use this concept because it's my favorite." Tell them *why* you think it works best and how it can offer them a competitive advantage. Give detailed reasoning for all your decisions and back them up with any design theory or working examples that use similar elements.

Treat each concept as a single entity. Spend the same amount of time explaining the thought process behind each concept and answer questions after explaining each concept. This way, the concepts won't become mixed up in the client's mind, and you're giving each concept equal weight.

## What if the client rejects every concept?

You can't always guarantee that the client will buy into your vision, even if you've actively given valid reasons for your decisions. Sometimes even referring to the brief as evidence that your solutions are relevant may not convince a client. You can persist by showing further exploration of the concept and application or carry out additional research into how you can back up your thinking.

Unfortunately, some clients will hold their ground and even the best salesperson in the world wouldn't be able to get through. If this happens to you, refer to the terms of your contract. For example, your contract may stipulate that if the designs you've created don't conform to the aims of the brief, then you're obliged to repeat the process at no extra cost. But if you feel you've met the aims of the design brief (and you can back this up), don't be tricked into repeating the process—some clients may try to use this as an opportunity to see more ideas for free.

**Remember:** Some clients are impossible to please—and often you don't know which clients will fall into this category when you get started. So, make sure you're covered in this situation by any contract you sign.

## DEALING WITH CLIENT FEEDBACK

After you present your concepts to your client, you want to get feedback. That's right—you *want* feedback. Without it, you won't know how the client feels, and you won't know whether you've met their needs.

Many designers dread client feedback—they see it as a battle of wills. But not all feedback is negative, and even negative feedback doesn't have to result in a battle. Your client may feel defensive if they don't like your concepts, but you can help ease that defensiveness by responding professionally and politely.

Nobody likes negative feedback. But the key is to push aside your ego and understand that it's not personal. Some of your clients may not be brimming with tact—unfortunately, not everyone understands that the best way to give criticism is to voice concerns constructively. If you feel like the client is insulting you personally, don't lose your cool.

**Remember:** Design is subjective. Your client may not fully understand that there is a certain degree of theory behind your design choices. If they have queries about any of your design choices, back up your ideas with reasonable examples of why they work and how alternative options wouldn't be as effective.

## REVISING

If you've overcome the hurdle of getting the client to buy into one of your concepts, then you're halfway there. They may fall in love with one right away, but odds are, they'll want to see some different versions of the concept.

A concept shouldn't be seen as a toy that a client can play around with until they think the logo looks great. Instead, you want to guide the client with sound design advice. That's not to say that all client suggestions will be wrong—some suggestions may improve the design. If that's the case, don't be reluctant to implement the changes just because you didn't think of them yourself. You can never explore a concept in too much detail, so presenting variations of an original idea can put your mind at ease that you're working with the client toward the best possible solution.

If the client suggests making a change that you know for sure won't work, explain why it won't work by giving valid reasons relating to your design knowledge. If you have the time, back it up by showing an example with the change implemented and an alternative that you know will be an improvement.

Even if the client falls in love with one of your concepts during the first round of presentation, don't rest on your laurels and assume that your work is done. Aim to take your ideas further and see if any additional improvements can be made. Your goal is to paint the client in the best possible light. Most designers will tell you that, when they look back on completed work, they see things they would do differently. You can reduce this possibility by fully exploring the potential for the final concept. Just make sure to keep the client updated on any changes you make. Trying to subtly sneak in a change without the client's approval is unprofessional. If you've made a change that you think improves the overall design, go back to the presentation process and explain why it has advantages over the previous version.

In 2010, I was contacted by Santa Clara Church to design their new identity. We decided that a modern icon should be used to help distance them from the stale, traditional images often associated with religion. The church adheres to four key values—connect, grow, serve, and go—and we felt that these values should somehow be reflected in the logo, possibly incorporating some kind of tree image with the four elements forming the branches. I presented Santa Clara with three concepts that conformed to this general idea (see Figure 11-9). Each concept was different, but all had some factor by which imagery or color was divided into four defined areas that symbolized each key value of the church.

After discussion, the client and I decided that learning about the four key values was similar to going on a journey onward and upward. We also decided that the key values shouldn't necessarily be illustrated literally but maybe in a more abstract fashion. After much thought, I presented the concept shown in Figure 11-10.

## When inspiration strikes

It's never too late to introduce new ideas. If you think of a groundbreaking idea at any stage in the design process, by all means present it to the client, even if you've already shared your initial concepts. If you've agreed to show only a certain number of concepts, don't allow that figure to put a stranglehold on your creativity.

Figure 11-9: The initial concepts that I presented to Santa Clara Church.

Figure 11-10: A revised concept based on discussion with and feedback from the client.

Notice how the artwork is not completely refined at this stage? Upon presentation, the client was onboard with the concept and the thinking behind it, and they loved the fact that the path formed a subliminal *S,* standing for Santa Clara Church. The four key values are symbolized by the four separate areas. From there, I worked with the client, experimenting with small changes in the measurements, position, and orientation of the elements used within the design, as well with typeface options (see Figure 11-11).

ORIGINAL

REVISIONS TO THE ICON

**1** Lightened the hue of the green area.

**2** Reduced amount of horizontal disposition. I suggest that the type should be underneath the icon rather than stacked beside it as it looks like two separate elements.

**3** Removed the horizontal disposition.

**4** Reversed the horizontal disposition.

**5** Redrew S/path/river with thicker stroke

**6** Removed the two tones on the colors. I think this decreases the depth and is less impactful.

149

Figure 11-11: Experimenting with a chosen concept.

Eventually, we were able to pinpoint the final design (see Figure 11-12).

Figure 11-12: The final Santa Clara Church logo, designed by Gareth Hardy (www.downwithdesign.com).

When you're all done with the design and you've gotten final approval from the client, ensure that you get written confirmation from the client. It doesn't have to be a formal letter—even an e-mail will suffice, just as long as you have something to refer to and show as proof if the client later tries to say that they want to go in a different direction. (You can even get the client to sign off at each stage of the process if you feel that's necessary.)

## What to do with unused ideas

In the process of designing a logo for a client, you'll come up with a variety of concepts that don't make the final cut. I'm not a fan of recycling concepts for future projects—each brief should be treated as an opportunity to create a brand-new solution. Still, hang on to every idea that you create—you never know when those unused ideas could come in handy, if only as inspiration for a new project.

If you look at logo showcase websites, you may notice that a majority of the concepts are rejected concepts. These websites offer designers exposure, but showcasing logo designs that your client rejected can be dangerous. Picture this scenario: A designer uploads to his portfolio and a logo-inspiration website several unused concepts for a business that is still actively operating. Numerous blogs and other logo-design-related websites pick up on the logo and decide to feature it in "inspirational" logo-design posts. The unused logo is now all over the Internet. If an Internet user searches for details on the client, all identities—the rejected ones and the one the client ultimately chose—could show up in the search results, which could cause conflict and damage the reputation of the brand.

Always ask for the client's permission to showcase any unused concepts—whether the client is still in business or not. If you feel that an unused logo concept will improve your portfolio, show just the mark and don't include any specific details about the client or the nature of the project. This protects the client's privacy.

Showcasing unused concepts, especially online, could lead to receiving enquiries for purchase of the copyright. Just because an idea got rejected doesn't mean that its value instantly drops. Great ideas are worth more than a couple hundred dollars, and they shouldn't be sold to just anyone. Think of the time and energy that went into developing the concept from the first idea in your head to the eventual execution of the artwork into vectors. If you do decide to sell unused ideas, make sure that the logo is suitable for the buyer's identity so that you maintain a high level professionalism as a designer.

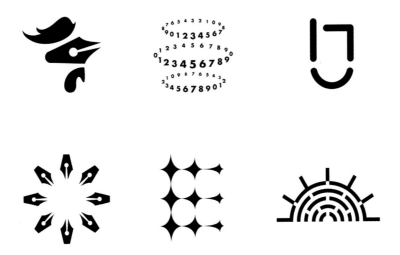

Some of my own unused concepts, with any identifying information about the clients removed.

# 12

# PREPARING SOURCE FILES

WITH THE CONCEPT approved, the next stage is crucial. Delivering the necessary files to the client is not as simple as giving them a nice, fresh printout of the work that you've created. The client needs to be able to use the files themselves, and the files need to be usable by anyone who needs to reproduce the logo in the future.

The final concept that the client approves during the presentation phase (see Chapter 11) probably will perform well once it's reproduced. But you should still test the logo to ensure that you

identify and rectify all potential errors. What exactly are you testing for? You want to make sure your logo looks wonderful not only when scaled down or displayed on-screen, but also when applied on a larger scale or different material. In this chapter, I walk you through the testing process.

In addition, with so many file types available to a designer, knowing which ones the client needs can be confusing. This chapter helps you decide which file types to send to your client.

# TESTING

In Chapter 6, at the stage of conceptualization, you tested to see whether your ideas work and whether they fulfill the aims set out in the brief. Now that your client's has approved your concept, you need to test whether the execution of your idea through the final artwork is as versatile as possible, so that it performs in all possible applications.

## COMPENSATING FOR COLOR REVERSAL

In Chapter 7, I suggested reversing the colors to see if doing so affects the artwork—and it probably will a bit. When viewing a white surface area on a black background, the mind creates an optical illusion: The positive space created by the logo looks slightly larger than it would on a white background.

When supplying files to a client, it's a good idea to provide them with different versions that can be used on both white and black backgrounds. After your logo design is finalized and approved by the client, you need to make adjustments to prevent this optical illusion on the black background from happening by offsetting the path by a millimeter or two (see Figure 12-1). This will keep both versions of the logo consistent.

To offset the stroke in Adobe Illustrator, you can do the following:

1. Select your artwork using the Direct Selection tool (V).
2. Choose Object → Path → Offset Path. The Offset Path dialog box appears.
3. Enter a negative measurement (for example, –0.1 mm) in the Offset text box. This will create a new path on top of your original artwork by which the path is slightly smaller.
4. Click OK.

You can now move your new offset path next to the original artwork for comparison. Experiment with the Offset measurement until you're confident that the white background and black background versions are as identical as possible.

Keep in mind that you'll need to go through this process for typography as well as shapes. Finally, you may find that you have to clean up the new offset path after it has been created.

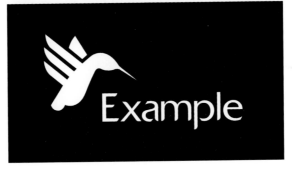

Figure 12-1: The original logo (top); the reversed logo not yet adjusted (middle); and the reversed logo adjusted to compensate for the optical illusion (bottom).

## PRINTING TO LOOK FOR ERRORS

Your monitor won't always reveal every error, so you should print your logo regularly as you make refinements and again at this final stage of file preparation (see Figure 12-2). A common problem is bleeding at smaller sizes if the artwork features tight areas of negative space.

I always print in black-and-white and then apply the colors later, because it's pretty pointless to test the correct values of colors using a standard inkjet printer. To get an exact idea of how your color choices will perform, no matter the material you're printing on, request a proof from the printer.

If the client mentions that they've printed out the logo and noticed that the color looks slightly different than it does on-screen, explain that the color modes still need to be adjusted. Also, keep in mind that the client's monitor may not be calibrated properly (see Chapter 10).

Figure 12-2: Test-printing the artwork.

Photo by Gareth Hardy

## CLEANING UP THE FILE

As you know, vectors are created using mathematically precise points. But unwanted points in the artwork could interfere with adjacent artwork down the road. The best method to check for stray points in Adobe Illustrator is to choose Select → All. This will reveal all the points currently within the document, if there are any. In Figure 12-3, I've circled the stray points.

You also need to ensure that your paths are closed properly (see Figure 12-4). An open path can cause problems for reproduction methods such as embroidery because it won't fully cover the whole of the intended line work. Select the path to see whether the path is closed.

Figure 12-3: Stray points.

Figure 12-4: Here the line is not completed even though the artwork appears to be a solid fill.

# Preparing different versions of the logo

As you experimented with the artwork at the layout and presentation stages, you may have noticed that the same orientation won't always be possible. For example, if the layout of the logo forms a landscape rectangular surface area, it may look awkward if the orientation of your artwork is portrait. Providing different layouts and orientations prevents the client from trying to alter the logo's layout or orientation themselves.

In addition, you may want to provide variations on the color of the logo. Standard color variations include the following:

- The main color version
- A grayscale version
- A black-and-white version
- One-color versions

## TESTING APPLICATION

Some logos need to be reproduced in different materials and using various methods. Examples include

- Embroidery
- Letterpress
- Color reproduction (for coated or uncoated stocks)

All this should be spelled out in the design brief (see Chapter 4).

If the client has any of these special requirements, you may need to make some slight changes to the file before it's sent to the printer. In some circumstances, you may need to provide a more simplified version of the logo, especially for letterpress.

## KNOWING WHICH FILE TYPES TO PROVIDE

Even some experienced designers don't know the purpose of the vast array of file types. Much to my amazement, some designers actually charge extra for supplying their clients with editable vector files of the logo; some even refuse to send the vector file at all, for fear that the client will make unapproved changes. What's the point in creating a logo using vectors if you won't let the client use it in that medium? A printer will at some point ask for the logo to be provided in vector format, so you need to provide that file to the client.

The next chapter explains how you can protect the original artwork, but before you do that, you need to know the right types of files to provide. The type of files you'll have to send the client depends on the design brief (see Chapter 4).

I always organize the files into two folders: print and screen. Within those folders, I create subfolders for each version of the logo.

## PRINT

To achieve optimal output, files for print need to be of a higher resolution than they do for the screen (at least 300 dpi for print). However, when you're dealing with vectors (the optimal file format for creating logos), the need for resolution is absent because they can be resized from the file that you provide.

When it comes to print, the following file types are your options:

- **EPS:** EPS stands for Encapsulated PostScript and is the common print-ready format. The EPS file is king, primarily because it can do most of the things that the other file formats can do. If you have the EPS file, you'll be able to export to other file extensions.
- **AI or CDR:** AI stands for Adobe Illustrator and CDR stands for CorelDRAW. Corel-DRAW is able to open and edit Adobe Illustrator files, but not all versions of Adobe Illustrator are able to handle CorelDRAW files. An advantage that CorelDRAW has is its ability to export to both AI and CDR.
- **PDF:** Portable Document Format is the standard file type for exchanging documents, so it's one that clients will likely be comfortable with. You can embed vector images within PDFs, and the artwork can be extracted from the PDF if required. If you export to PDF, you may want to put a password on the ability to edit the vector artwork contained within the PDF. This prevents anyone who receives the file from gaining access to the source files. You can send both print-ready and screen-ready versions of a PDF, as PDFs can contain raster graphics as well as vector graphics.

Most vector programs are able to read EPS as editable files, but it's always beneficial to have the original AI or CDR file available as a backup in case the EPS isn't compatible with a future user's software. From the AI or CDR file, you'll be able to create an EPS.

## SCREEN

Files intended for the use on-screen should be saved at a resolution of 72 dpi. The dimensions of the file depends on the size of the screen and the intended usage. When providing files intended primarily for the screen, I often provide them at different sizes to prevent the client from affecting the proportions of the artwork when attempting to rescale. When preparing files for screen output, you can use Adobe Illustrator to export to some compatible formats, but for use on the web, you'll find that you have to import the artwork into Adobe Photoshop and save from there.

Here are the file types I send (as a minimum) for use on-screen:

- **PNG:** Portable Network Graphics files offer the ability to export using varying levels of transparency, which can come in handy if the client needs to publish the logo to the Internet. PNGs also have the capacity to handle line work when an Internet browser resizes it.

- **GIF:** Graphics Interchange Format was specifically created for use on the Internet. GIFs are capable of supporting up to 256 colors selected from RGB output. If GIFs aren't used carefully, though, quality can be lost—make sure that the quality of the GIF is set to No Dither and that the colors are set to 256.

- **JPEG:** One of the best ways to reduce file sizes is to use the Joint Photographic Experts Group format because it can compress the data without significantly losing any of the quality. JPEG is the file type that most clients automatically assume they should use for everything concerning the logo, just because it's a file type most people are familiar with.

## SPECIAL REQUESTS

Sometimes, clients need logos in a particular format, beyond the types listed in the previous two sections. Here are the most common types of file requested:

- **PSD:** In my experience, the most common request is for the logo to be supplied in PSD (Photoshop) format. Usually, when clients request the PSD file, they're hoping to play around with the colors and ruin all your hard work. If a client asks for the PSD file, explain that there is no need for a PSD because you supply the final artwork. If the client needs a different color or variation, provide it to them in the relevant file formats, not in PSD. If they won't settle for anything other than a PSD, you might supply a flattened PSD to keep them happy.

- **TIFF:** TIFF, which stands for Tagged Image File Format, is supported by many publishing programs. Like PSDs, TIFFs can store layers, so the client can hand a TIFF over to any designers who work with the logo in the future.

## Fonts

"Can you please send us the font used in the logo?"

How would you tackle this question? It may seem like the obvious thing to do is to hand over the font. But most clients don't understand that, to use a font, you need a license. Even if you paid for the font and have a valid license for its usage, that license may cover only one user. If you're using a font, refer back to where you acquired it and check the license agreement. You'll probably need an additional license. If so, you can buy this on the client's behalf and add the costs to the final bill, or tell the client where they can buy it for themselves.

- **BMP:** I'm not joking, but I wish I were. A Bitmap image file is a raster graphic that is commonly used by Microsoft publishing packages. BMPs are often easier to work with if collateral such as letterheads are being created using Microsoft Word, but in general, they print poorly and should be avoided whenever possible.

- **PPT:** You'd be surprised by how many clients are unable to complete the simple task of importing a JPEG into a PowerPoint presentation. I often provide a single screen template in a PPT file that contains the logo so that the client doesn't reduce the quality of the output of the logo if they plan to give presentations.

## Archiving your work

I always keep an extra backup of all the files I create for a client, whether they're logos or something else. Technology is unreliable—it can be damaged at any time without warning, usually when you need it the most. Having an extra copy of files ensures that they won't be lost forever if a disaster occurs. Plus, you can't trust a client not to lose or damage the copies of the files you sent them. Copying the deliverables to an extra hard drive or to disc offers an extra level of security.

# 13

# SETTING LOGO USAGE GUIDELINES

THE LOGO IS complete, now what? Do you just let the client ride off into the sunset with your design and let them slap the logo on anything they want? The answer is no, not without guidance to ensure that the identity you've created remains consistent. Your involvement in a logo design doesn't end when the files are ready to be given to the client. The final stage in the process is setting logo usage guidelines.

If you've designed logos in the past, the client may have made some changes to your final artwork after you handed over the deliverables. They might have added a new obscure font because "we found it online and it looks really cool!" They might have even changed the colors because they think "it pops." Seeing your work treated in such a way can be demoralizing (not to mention ruin the identity you created), but you can prevent these situations with logo usage guidelines.

Logo usage guidelines will be useful to anyone who needs to use the logo, now or in the future—including other professionals within the creative industry. The client may hire another designer or design team down the road; if so, the client should give the new designer your logo usage guidelines to make sure that his decisions conform to the identity. Printers also may refer to the guidelines if they're not sure which color reproduction method to use and which inks to select.

# THE PURPOSE OF LOGO USAGE GUIDELINES

Imagine you've just purchased a new piece of technology. In the box, you find a detailed instruction manual that tells you how to use the device. Logo usage guidelines are no different—they're a way for you, the designer, to communicate to your client how to use the logo you've designed for them.

Logo usage guidelines offer the following benefits:

- **They help to guide and educate anyone who uses the logo about the design choices you made.** Most of your clients won't have a design background, so they may not realize that every decision you made when it comes to the logo was made for a specific reason. If they're aware of how much thought went into your design, they'll be less likely to tinker with it.
- **They improve the efficiency and consistency for any future design work carried out using the logo.** If, down the road, any design professionals need to work with the logo, regardless of the medium, you can be assured that the brand identity will remain consistent.
- **They help to ensure regulated reproduction both on-screen and in print.** Providing different color values for at least RGB and CMYK ensures that the output for each medium will look as similar as possible.
- **They provide a more professional service and package for the client.** When you design a logo and e-mail it off with a simple "Nice working with you!," you're not communicating the same message as you are when you include detailed logo usage guidelines. If you provide guidelines on the logo's usage, the client will see you as the professional designer you are and respect the work you've done.
- **They prevent possible design disasters that are beyond your control.** This includes printers playing around with the dimensions or color values used in the logo, or clients applying the logo in such a way that it isn't even close to the original design that you created.
- **They enhance competitive advantage.** Usage guidelines ensure that the identity remains regulated, which will in turn make it look more professional than the identities of competitors who don't employ logo usage guidelines.

Consistency is key when it comes to brand identity, and logo usage guidelines help your client to achieve that consistency for years to come. Have you ever noticed that the logos of the world's biggest brands always look the same, no matter where you see them? Whether you're looking at the Coca-Cola logo on the side of a can or on a roadside billboard, the logo looks the same. This isn't a coincidence.

Part of what you want to do in working with your client—from the beginning of the design process to the end—is sell them on the importance of consistency. That way, when you present the client with the logo usage guidelines, you can remind them that this document will help them achieve the same consistency that the world's biggest brands achieve.

A consistent brand identity increases recognition. A logo that's used inconsistently can cause confusion for the audience. Logo usage guidelines help to provide a springboard for future brand development and identity exploration and adaptation. They're the basis for, rather than the overall scope of, the rules and regulations concerning the visual identity.

## ESSENTIAL COMPONENTS

I've sold you on the purpose and importance of logo usage guidelines. So, now all you need to know is what to include in the guidelines you write. In this section, I walk you through the contents. For readability, I recommend that each of these components be given its own page in your document.

*Note:* If you're designing a brand, not just a logo, you'll probably need to design brand guidelines instead. Those will be much more detailed, including elements that go way beyond the logo. Brand guidelines include specifications for logo usage. Even if someone else is working on the wider brand identity, you should provide advice for optimal visual performance of the logo.

### FRONT COVER

A front cover, which clearly explains the purpose of the document and contains the logo, helps distinguish your guidelines from the average piece of office paperwork (see Figure 13-1).

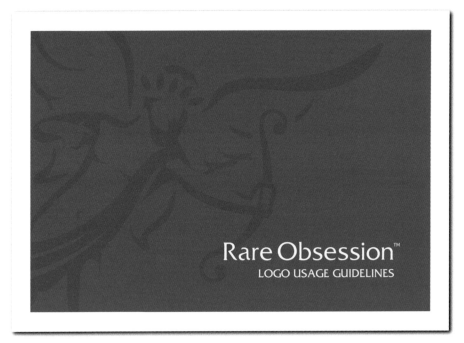

Figure 13-1: The front cover.

## TABLE OF CONTENTS

Including a table of contents helps people find the information they're looking for. Your goal is to make the guidelines as easy to use and understand as possible, and a table of contents helps you reach that goal (see Figure 13-2).

## BRANDMARK

Clients don't always realize that the whole artwork provided for the creation of the logo is the defined artwork that should not be tampered with. The brandmark section of your guidelines (see Figure 13-3) should

- Confirm the exact elements of the logo
- Explain that, if type is used in the logo, it is not a font but an original piece of artwork, and should not be replaced by using a font
- Confirm that the dimensions of the artwork should not be changed

# Contents

Figure 13-2: The table of contents.

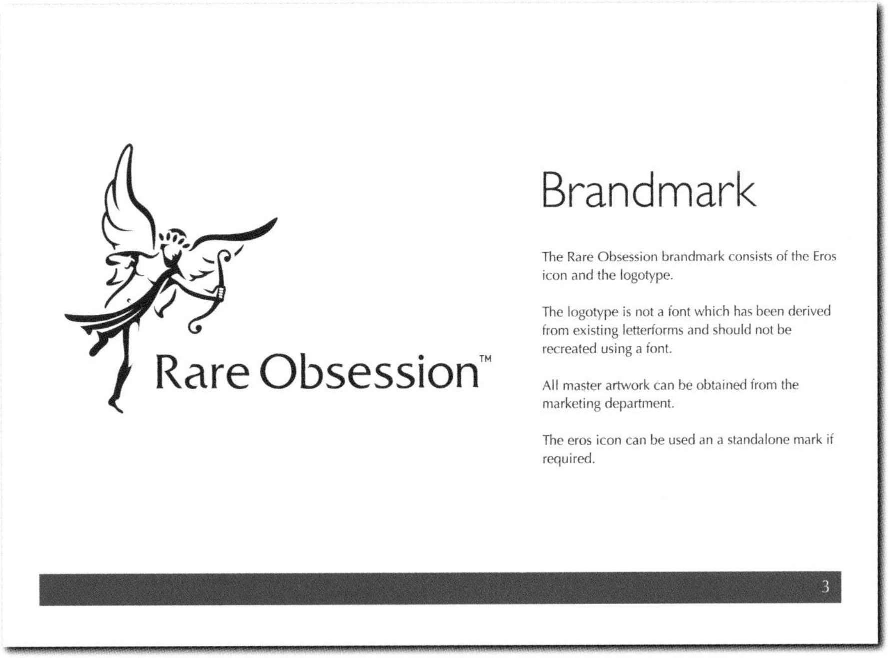

167

# Brandmark

The Rare Obsession brandmark consists of the Eros icon and the logotype.

The logotype is not a font which has been derived from existing letterforms and should not be recreated using a font.

All master artwork can be obtained from the marketing department.

The eros icon can be used an a standalone mark if required.

3

Figure 13-3: What is classed as the official logo.

## MINIMUM SIZE

If the logo is decreased in size too much, it won't be recognizable to the human eye. A logo that cannot be recognized is pointless. That minimum size is different for every logo, but the average minimum size is 45 millimeters for the whole brand mark. If your logo uses only an icon, as is this case for Apple, then the minimum size may be smaller. Be sure to define the minimum size in your logo usage guidelines (see Figure 13-4).

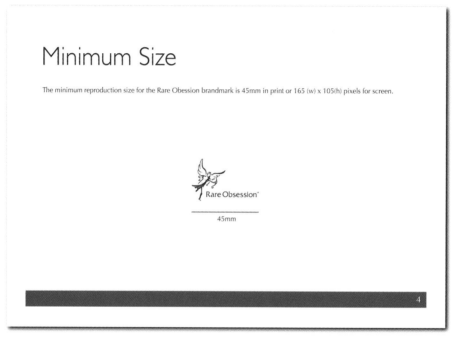

Figure 13-4: The smallest size at which the logo can be reproduced.

## CLEAR SPACE

Clear space (also known as white space) is your friend. Imagine a situation where numerous logos are shown in one given space—for example, on the sponsorship board for an event. Each logo is screaming out for attention, and if they're all extremely close together, the audience will have trouble recognizing each brand individually.

A minimum amount of clear space should be defined so that the logo has room to breathe and is easily identifiable in its own right, wherever it appears. This defined clear space helps to protect the integrity of the brand not only from competing logos but also from any assisting graphics, copy, or photography. The clear space should be proportionally maintained as the logo is increased or decreased in size. Giving an exact measurement in figures will be harder to work out, so minimum clear space often is measured in proportion, using an element of the logo for reference (see Figure 13-5).

Figure 13-5: The minimum clear space that should be allowed from the logo artwork.

## BACKGROUNDS

The logo may need to be reproduced on different types of backgrounds, so you should give guidelines for the following (see Figure 13-6):

- Whether a background color is part of the main logo
- Flat color options for background or gradients, if required
- Whether a photograph may be used as a background

## Backgrounds

For maximum impact it is recommended that the brandmark is used on a white background.

The brandmark can also be used on a coloured background selected from the colours provided in this document.

The brandmark should not be used near distracting elements or on busy background images.

6

Figure 13-6: Logo usage on different backgrounds.

## COLOR

In Chapter 7, I explained that there are different types of output for color, so in the logo usage guidelines, you should provide the different values for each medium and method. You can't assume that the client will always be able to print using Pantones, so you should also provide four-color process values.

Provide color values in the following formulas:

- **RGB:** For screen usage composed of red, green, and blue
- **Hex:** For use on the web
- **Pantones:** For printing with Pantone inks
- **CMYK:** For four-color process printing comprised of cyan, magenta, yellow, and black, when Pantones are not available

Provide instructions for the use of each different color output—your client may not have heard of them (see Figure 13-7).

Figure 13-7: The color values of different color modes and printing methods.

## SECONDARY PALETTE

You may want to provide examples of how other colors can be used to help support the logo (see Figure 13-8), but this isn't required—it's more relevant to brand identity guidelines. Even if you aren't designing the whole brand identity, you can still make suggestions about what colors to use. This will help prevent the client or another design team from making a choice that conflicts with all your previous decisions.

## INCORRECT USAGE

There are right ways and wrong ways to use a logo. Show as many incorrect uses as possible so that you clearly communicate what can and can't be done (see Figure 13-9). In particular, be sure to show examples of incorrect usage concerning:

- Scale and perspective
- Color
- Orientation

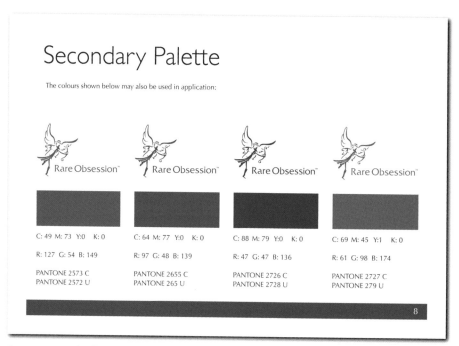

Figure 13-8: Examples of optional colors.

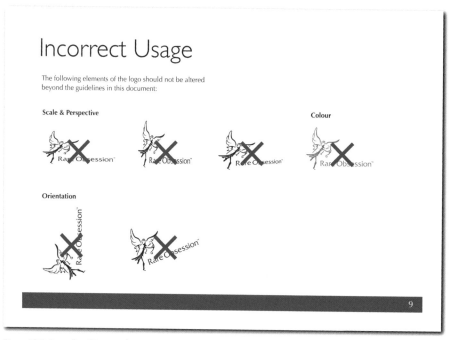

Figure 13-9: Examples of incorrect logo usage.

## The format of the guidelines: Screen or print?

What output should the logo usage guidelines be designed for: screen or print? Designing for print is common sense, because the resolution won't affect how the logo looks on-screen.

I always provide the guidelines in both hard copy and as a digital file that can be shared easily with future users. This way, the client can always reproduce copies of the guidelines down the road. As with the logo source files themselves, keep a copy of the guidelines so that you can update the guidelines in the future, if necessary.

# 14

# AVOIDING COMMON LOGO DESIGN MISTAKES

IN THE PREVIOUS chapters, I've outlined the steps to take when designing a logo, and what you need to do in order for your logo to be successful. Not all logo designers follow the same process, but the final product is the same: a logo.

In this chapter, I summarize some common mistakes that logo designers make. Before you get started designing a logo, review this chapter to remind yourself what *not* to do. After you finish your logo, review this chapter again and assess whether you were successful in side-stepping these potential pitfalls.

## USING RASTER GRAPHICS

The standard practice when designing a logo is to use vector graphics software, such as Adobe Illustrator or Corel Draw. A vector graphic is made up of mathematically precise points and provides visual consistency at multiple sizes. On the other hand, a raster graphic (or bitmap as they're commonly called), made with raster graphic software such as Adobe Photoshop, consists of pixels.

The use of raster images in logos can cause problems for reproduction (see Figure 14-1). You can create a high-resolution raster graphic logo, but you don't know for sure how large that logo will need to be reproduced. If you zoom in on a raster graphic, it will eventually appear pixilated, rendering it impractical. A logo must look the same at all sizes to maintain visual recognition.

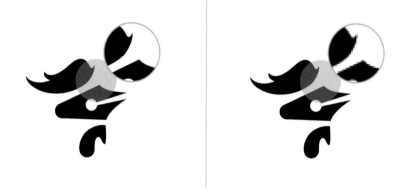

Figure 14-1: An example of how raster graphics can limit reproduction. On the left is a vector graphic; on the right, a raster graphic.

Vector graphics can be scaled at any size without losing quality and can be applied to other design media easier than raster images can. Plus, vector graphics make editing the logo at a later stage a much easier process.

## USING STOCK ART

This mistake is often made by business owners trying to design their own logos or by amateur designers who aren't aware of copyright laws. Downloading stock vector imagery from websites is not a crime, but it can get you into a lot of trouble if you decide to implement it into a logo.

A logo should be unique and original, with the license agreement being exclusive to the client. Using stock art breaks this rule. Plus, chances are, if you use a stock vector graphic, it's being used somewhere else in the world, so the logo won't be unique. You can easily spot a stock vector graphic in a logo—they're often familiar shapes such as globes or silhouettes (see Figure 14-2).

**Stock Globe**
Downloaded: 300,000 times.

**VECTOR ILLUSTRATION**  $10

ADD TO SWAG

You have 0 Credibility

View More Like This?

Figure 14-2: Using stock vector graphics in a logo can put your client at risk.

## DESIGNING FOR YOURSELF RATHER THAN THE CLIENT

I can spot this design sin a mile off. It's usually the result of the designer having an enormous ego. If there's a cool new font that you love and you can't wait to use it in your design, well, don't. Is that font really appropriate for your client's business? Your idea for a great modern typographic solution probably isn't suitable for a serious business such as solicitors (see Figure 14-3).

Figure 14-3: You should never input your own personality into a client's work.

Some designers also make the mistake of including their "recognizable style" in their work. You should be proud of your work, but putting your own personality into a logo is wrong. Stay focused on the client's requirements by sticking to the brief.

## RELYING ON TRENDS

Trends come and go, and they ultimately end up as clichés. A well-designed logo should be timeless. You can achieve this timelessness by ignoring the latest design trick or gimmick.

The most common cliché in logo design is the dreaded "corporate swoosh" (see Figure 14-4), which is the ultimate way to play it safe.

Figure 14-4: Focusing on current logo trends puts a sell-by date on a logo.

As a logo designer, your job is to create a unique identity for your client, so you should completely ignore logo design trends. Not sure what the latest trends are? Go to LogoLounge (`www.logolounge.com`) and click on Trend Reports at the bottom of the page. You'll find a report on the current logo design trends, updated annually. As a designer, you need to be aware of the latest craze . . . so that you can avoid it at all costs.

## BEING TOO COMPLEX

Take a look at your finger—you'll notice that you can see the detail of your fingerprint only when it's really close to your face. If you move your finger away, you can no longer see the fingerprint. The same rule applies to highly detailed logo designs.

When printed, a complex design will lose detail at smaller sizes, and in some cases, it may look like a smudge or a mistake (see Figure 14-5). When a logo is more detailed, there is more information for the viewer to acknowledge. A great logo should be memorable, and the best way to achieve this is to keep things simple. Take a look at the corporate identities of Nike, McDonald's, and Apple—they're simple icons, easily reproduced at any size, and very memorable.

Figure 14-5: Highly detailed designs are unlikely to scale well when printed or viewed at smaller sizes.

# FAILING TO PROVIDE A SOLUTION IN THE ABSENCE OF COLOR

Some designers can't wait to start adding color to a design, and some logos even rely on color completely. Choosing color should be the last decision—you're always better off starting your work in black and white.

In some situations, a logo will need to be reproduced in one color, so you should be sure to test your design to see if this affects the identity. If color helps to identify certain elements of the design, it will look completely different in one tone (see Figure 14-6). Always provide a version of the design in one color to avoid future reproduction complications.

179

Figure 14-6: In the absence of color, your great design might lose it's identity.

## CHOOSING THE WRONG TYPEFACE

When it comes to executing a logo concept, choosing the right font is the most important decision a designer can make. More often than not, a logo will be let down by a poor font choice (see Figure 14-7).

Figure 14-7: Typeface choices can make or break a logo.

Finding the perfect font for your design is all about matching the style of the icon, but this can be tricky. If the match is too good, the mark and font compete with each other for visual attention. If it doesn't match at all, then the viewer won't know where to focus. The key is achieving the right balance. Each typeface has a personality; if the font you choose doesn't reflect the characteristics of the mark, then the brand message won't be communicated effectively.

Designers tend to choose the wrong font when they don't take the decision seriously enough. Some designers simply throw the type in as an afterthought. (For much more on choosing a font, turn to Chapter 8.)

## USING TOO MANY FONTS

Using too many fonts is like trying to show someone a whole photo album all at once. Each typeface looks different, and the viewer needs time to recognize each one—seeing too many all at once can cause confusion (see Figure 14-8).

It's standard practice to use a maximum of two fonts or two weights. Restricting the amount of fonts in a logo design can greatly improve the legibility and increase brand recognition.

Figure 14-8: The number of fonts on the left makes the logo harder to read.

## PLAGIARIZING

Plagiarizing is the biggest logo design mistake of all, and, unfortunately, it's becoming more and more common. The main purpose of a logo is to identify a business. If a company's logo looks the same as another company's logo, the logo fails. Copying someone else does nobody any favors—including the designer.

III

**PART**

# SHOWCASE

15

# PICTORIAL MARKS

THIS CHAPTER SHOWCASES logo designs that use pictorial marks. Pictorial marks can be identified as recognizable and familiar images. Because they're so familiar, pictorial marks make an instant connection with the viewer. They draw on people's experiences and association with the image in order to link that image to the brand. The image is often related to a number of characteristics of the entity that it identifies, including the brand name.

**MEMORYWASH**

**Memory Wash**

**Designer:** Leighton Hubbell (California, United States)

**Web:** www.leightonhubbell.com

**Taurus Construction**

**Designer:** Mike Erickson (California, United States)

**Web:** www.logomotive.net

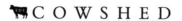

**cinemacafé**

**The Cowshed Bar and Grill**

**Designer:** JamFactory (Bristol, England)

**Web:** www.jam-factory.com

**cinemacafé**

**Designer:** Muamer Adilovic (Sarajevo, Bosnia, and Herzegovina)

**Web:** www.muameradilovic.com

**LOCKSLEY
WEST**

**Profis Bud**
*Piękno płynie z Natury*

**Locksley West**

**Designer:** Jan Zabransky (Zlin,
Czech Republic)

**Web:** www.janzabransky.cz

**Profis Bud**

**Designer:** Midgar.eu (Grabownica,
Poland)

**Web:** www.midgar.eu

*187*

**COLORADO
CONSERVATION
TRUST**

**Colorado Conservation Trust**

**Designer:** Glen Hobbs/Logoboom
(Colorado, United States)

**Colibry**

**Designer:** This Is Nido (Birmingham,
England)

**Web:** www.thisisnido.com

**Industrial Wisdom**

**Designer:** Glen Hobbs/Logoboom
(Colorado, United States)

**petfoto**

**Designer:** Uneek Grafix (Illinois,
United States)

**Web:** www.uneekgrafix.com

188

**Galaxy Garden**

**Designer:** James Strange (Nebraska,
United States)

**Bio-Mechanical**

**Designer:** Josh Hayes (Victoria, Australia)

**Web:** www.hayesimage.com.au

**Queen's Glass**

**Designer:** Andrei Gadoiu (Bihor, Romania)

**Web:** www.fivetailors.com

**Caballo**

**Designer:** Oguzhan Ocalan (Hanau, Germany)

**Web:** www.gravitart.com

**Aquasis**

**Designer:** James Strange (Nebraska, United States)

**Inspire to Success!**

**Designer:** Glen Hobbs/Logoboom (Colorado, United States)

# LIMELIGHT
### STUDIOS

**Limelight Studios**

**Designer:** Sean Farrell (Michigan, United States)

**Web:** www.brandclay.com

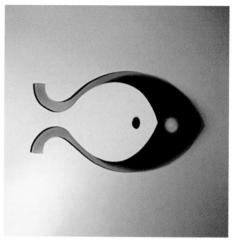

**Seablings Fish Market**

**Designer:** Rudy Hurtado (Ontario, Canada)

**Web:** www.rudyhurtado.com

47. revija hrvatskog
filmskog i
videostvaralaštva
djece

**47th Festival**

**Designer:** Type08 (Koprivnica, Croatia)

**Web:** www.type08.com

# MEMORY
# LANE®

**Memory Lane**

**Designer:** Glen Hobbs/Logoboom (Colorado, United States)

**Al Qasr**

**Designer:** Ghiath Lahham (Dubai, United Arab Emirates)

**Web:** www.ghiathlahham.com

**Prima Donna Luxury Jewels**

**Designer:** Andrei Gadoiu (Bihor, Romania)

**Web:** www.fivetailors.com

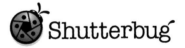

**Bowes of Norfolk**

**Designer:** Roy Smith (Norwich, England)

**Web:** www.roysmithdesign.com

**Shutterbug**

**Designer:** Jerron Ames (Utah, United States)

**Conagra Foods**

**Designer:** James Strange (Nebraska, United States)

**Grace Hospice**

**Designer:** James Strange (Nebraska, United States)

**Nebraska AIDS Project**

**Designer:** Oxide Design Co. (Nebraska, United States)

**Web:** www.oxidedesign.com

**Anglers Association**

**Designer:** Galin Kastelov (Sofia, Bulgaria)

**Web:** www.kastelov.com

**Fight Torture**

**Designer:** Lorena Mirbach (Hamburg, Germany)

**Uncork'd**

**Designer:** Randy Heil (Arizona, United States)

**Web:** www.randyheil.com

**Swan**

**Designer:** Peter Vasvari (Karokatona, Hungary)

**Web:** www.petervasvari.com

**Honey Bee**

**Designer:** Peter Vasvari (Karokatona, Hungary)

**Web:** www.petervasvari.com

RANDALL
MUSEUM

**Randall Museum**

**Designer:** Inka Mathew/Green Ink Studio
(Texas, United States)

**Web:** www.greeninkstudio.com

**Power Line**

**Designer:** James Strange (Nebraska,
United States)

elephruit

GRAIN HOUSE
Agricultural Company

**Elephruit**

**Designer:** This Is Nido (Birmingham,
England)

**Web:** www.thisisnido.com

**Grain House**

**Designer:** Nikita Lebedev (Kostroma,
Russia)

**Hand Crafted in Canada**

**Designer:** Rudy Hurtado (Ontario, Canada)

**Web:** www.rudyhurtado.com

**Kosher Wine Express**

**Designer:** Euan MacKenzie (East Kilbride, Scotland)

**Web:** www.euanmackenzie.com

195

**Griffin**

**Designer:** John Neiner (Massachusetts, United States)

**Web:** www.neinercreative.com

**Cadoba Poduha**

**Designer:** Alexander Badovsky (Kiev, Ukraine)

**Web:** www.badovsky.com

**Muddy Boots Landscaping**

**Designer:** Sean Farrell (Michigan, United States)

**Web:** www.brandclay.com

196

**Green Rail**

**Designer:** James Strange (Nebraska, United States)

**Piraap Publishers**

**Designer:** Attak ('s-Hertegosenbasch, The Netherlands)

**Web:** www.attakweb.com

**Grassland Grains & Kitchens**

**Designer:** Josiah Jost (Alberta, Canada)

**Web:** www.siahdesign.com

**TravelWorld**

**Designer:** Brandberry (Samara, Russia)

**Web:** www.brandberry.net

**Envision**

**Designer:** Randy Heil (Arizona, United States)

**Web:** www.randyheil.com

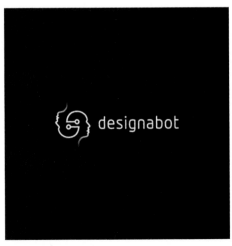

**Designabot**

**Designer:** Rich Scott (Queensland, Australia)

**Web:** www.designabot.net

**Lady Shocking Revelation**

**Designer:** 903 Creative (Virgina, United States)

**Web:** www.903creative.com

**Blue Mountain Electric, LLC**

**Designer:** Sean Farrell (Michigan, United States)

**Web:** www.brandclay.com

**H&C Inso**

**Designer:** Wizemark (Backa Palanka, Serbia)

**Web:** www.wizemark.com

**EuroYacht**

**Designer:** The Logo Factory (Ontario, Canada)

**Web:** www.thelogofactory.com

**Toreto**

**Designer:** Oronoz Brandesign (Chihuahua, Mexico)

**Web:** www.alanoronoz.com

## Exotiq

**Designer:** Me and Mister Jones (Antwerp, Belgium)

**Web:** www.meandmisterjones.com

## Caritas

**Designer:** Inka Mathew/Green Ink Studio (Texas, United States)

**Web:** www.greeninkstudio.com

*199*

## Imported Mexican Foods

**Designer:** Sneh Roy (Sydney, Australia)

**Web:** www.littleboxofideas.com

## Dig for Saint Michaels

**Designer:** Gareth Hardy (Birmingham, England)

**Web:** www.downwithdesign.com

**Bee**

**Designer:** A. William Patino (Guaymallen, Argentina)

**Jungpark**

**Designer:** Gareth Hardy (Birmingham, England)

**Web:** www.downwithdesign.com

**Hombre Mexican Restaurant**

**Designer:** Type08 (Koprivnica, Croatia)

**Web:** www.type08.com

**Excalibur**

**Designer:** Randy Heil (Arizona, United States)

**Web:** www.randyheil.com

**Big Kahuna Software**

**Designer:** Jerron Ames (Utah, United States)

**Fashion Hair Stylist**

**Designer:** Muamer Adilovic (Sarajevo, Bosnia & Herzegovina)

**Web:** www.muameradilovic.com

201

**Biohof Angern**

**Designer:** Lorena Mirbach (Hamburg, Germany)

**Mikazuki Camera**

**Designer:** Gareth Hardy (Birmingham, England)

**Web:** www.downwithdesign.com

**Youfashion.com**

**Designer:** Oronoz Brandesign (Chihuahua, Mexico)

**Web:** www.alanoronoz.com

**Tullamore Estate**

**Designer:** Koodoz Design (Victoria, Australia)

**Web:** www.koodoz.com.au

# 16

# ABSTRACT AND SYMBOLIC MARKS

THIS CHAPTER SHOWCASES abstract and symbolic marks, those that are not instantly identifiable. The abstract nature of the mark may intrigue the viewer, with the graphic often representing a brand feeling, attribute, or value. Often, the simplicity of the graphic increases the chances of an abstract and symbolic mark remaining truly timeless.

LAURUS NOBILIS

**Laurus Nobilis**

**Designer:** John Neiner (Massachusetts, United States)

**Web:** www.neinercreative.com

**Handel Group**

**Designer:** Carrihan Creative Group/ Christopher Hanley (Texas, United States)

**Web:** www.carrihan.com

**CitiSync**

**Designer:** Mike Erickson (California, United States)

**Web:** www.logomotive.net

**Peaceful Healings**

**Designer:** Raja Sandhu (Ontario, Canada)

**Web:** www.rajasandhu.com

**Mobileactive.org**

**Designer:** Brandsimplicity (Maddington, Australia)

**Web:** www.brandsimplicity.com.au

**Wire to Ear Recording Co.**

**Designer:** Brent Couchman Design (California, United States)

**Web:** www.brentcouchman.com

**Stereo**

**Designer:** Mister (Glasgow, Scotland)

**Web:** www.studiomister.com

**Euphonic**

**Designer:** Kevin Burr (Tennessee, United States)

**Web:** www.ocularink.com

**Iconik**

**Designer:** Type08 (Koprivnica, Croatia)

**Web:** www.type08.com

**Cart**

**Designer:** Mister (Glasgow, Scotland)

**Web:** www.studiomister.com

**Spice Mountain**

**Designer:** Made By Thomas (West Vlaanderen, Belgium)

**Web:** www.madebythomas.com

**Urban Acres**

**Designer:** Brandberry (Samara, Russia)

**Web:** www.brandberry.net

**Pinacia**

**Designer:** The Logo Factory (Ontario, Canada)

**Web:** www.thelogofactory.com

**Raam Audio**

**Designer:** Euan MacKenzie (East Kilbride, Scotland)

**Web:** www.euanmackenzie.com

*207*

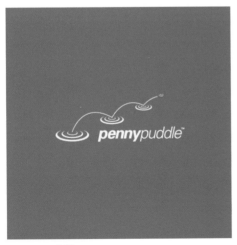

**pennypuddle**

**Designer:** Rich Scott (Queensland, Australia)

**Web:** www.designabot.net

**Amari**

**Designer:** Milou (Cieszyn, Poland)

**Web:** www.milou.com.pl

**David Lammens**

**Designer:** Made By Thomas (West Vlaanderen, Belgium)

**Web:** www.madebythomas.com

**Silent Progression**

**Designer:** FX3/Julien Gionis (Athens, Greece)

**Web:** www.fx3.gr

**Contre**

**Designer:** Milou (Cieszyn, Poland)

**Web:** www.milou.com.pl

**Incendio**

**Designer:** Raja Sandhu (Ontario, Canada)

**Web:** www.rajasandhu.com

**Dukat**

**Designer:** Cris Labno (Cracow, Poland)

**Web:** www.crislabno.com

**Soren Fund Management**

**Designer:** James Strange (Nebraska, United States)

**Lemon8**

**Designer:** This Is Nido (Birmingham, England)

**Web:** www.thisisnido.com

**Sunparks**

**Designer:** Lorena Mirbach (Hamburg, Germany)

**Promantek**

**Designer:** Brandberry (Samara, Russia)

**Web:** www.brandberry.net

**Showcatcher**

**Designer:** Sean O'Grady (County Mayo, Ireland)

**Web:** www.fogradesign.com

**Worldonline**

**Designer:** This Is Nido (Birmingham, England)

**Web:** www.thisisnido.com

**Museum of Japanese Balance**

**Designer:** Milou (Cieszyn, Poland)

**Web:** www.milou.com.pl

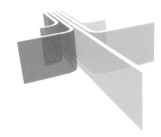

**Koolajong Australia**

**Designer:** Jerron Ames (Utah, United States)

**Excellence in Manufacturing**

**Designer:** Matthew Harpin (Rotherham, England)

**Web:** www.brand-design.co.uk

**Regional Business Center**

**Designer:** Brandberry (Samara, Russia)

**Web:** www.brandberry.net

**Printstunt.nl**

**Designer:** Tim Boelaars (Amsterdam, The Netherlands)

**Web:** www.timboelaars.nl

**Handmade Cafe**

**Designer:** Sergey Shapiro (Moscow, Russia)

**Web:** www.fromtheska.ru

212

**Moorland Associates**

**Designer:** Gareth Hardy (Birmingham, England)

**Web:** www.downwithdesign.com

**Lange Transport**

**Designer:** Lukasz Ruszel (Grabownica, Poland)

**Web:** www.midgar.eu

**The Sweetest Days**

**Designer:** Euan MacKenzie (East Kilbride, Scotland)

**Web:** www.euanmackenzie.com

**Kagawa Systems**

**Designer:** Lorena Mirbach (Hamburg, Germany)

**Godiva Books**

**Designer:** Gareth Hardy (Birmingham, England)

**Web:** www.downwithdesign.com

213

**Worldwide Wine**

**Designer:** Rich Scott (Queensland, Australia)

**Web:** www.designabot.net

# 17 WORDMARKS

THIS CHAPTER SHOWCASES wordmarks, logos that consist of one or more words. More often than not, the word is the name of the entity that the logo represents. A wordmark can be a simple typographic representation that stands alone, or it can includes an image inline with or replacing one or more letters. The designers featured in this chapter have chosen a defined typographic style, which helps to create an emotion or attitude that can be recognized by the viewer.

**Jiggle Eye Productions**

**Designer:** John Neiner (Massachusetts, United States)

**Web:** www.neinercreative.com

**Top Spot**

**Designer:** Wizemark (Backa Palanka, Serbia)

**Web:** www.wizemark.com

**Embloc**

**Designer:** Mister (Glasgow, Scotland)

**Web:** www.studiomister.com

**Threeleaves**

**Designer:** Sean O'Grady (County Mayo, Ireland)

**Web:** www.fogradesign.com

## Red

**Designer:** Sean Farrell (Michigan, United States)

**Web:** www.brandclay.com

ZEROWORK

## Zerowork

**Designer:** Anthony Lane (Minnesota, United States)

**Web:** www.012485.com

217

## Cocktails on Main

**Designer:** Galin Kastelov (Sofia, Bulgaria)

**Web:** www.kastelov.com

Jumeirah

## Jumeirah

**Designer:** Ghiath Lahham (Dubai, United Arab Emirates)

**Web:** www.ghiathlahham.com

**Wave**

**Designer:** Jan Zabransky (Zlin, Czech Republic)

**Web:** www.janzabransky.cz

**Akcent**

**Designer:** Mel Campbell (California, United States)

**Web:** www.six17.net

**Elastique**

**Designer:** Rich Scott (Queensland, Australia)

**Web:** www.designabot.net

**The Village Experience**

**Designer:** Roy Smith (Norwich, England)

**Web:** www.roysmithdesign.com

**Bamboo**

**Designer:** Craig Russell (Victoria, Australia)

**Botania**

**Designer:** Josiah Jost (Alberta, Canada)

**Web:** www.siahdesign.com

*219*

**Chronic Addiction**

**Designer:** Oguzhan Ocalan (Hanau, Germany)

**Web:** www.gravitart.com

**Colab**

**Designer:** Mister (Glasgow, Scotland)

**Web:** www.studiomister.com

**Panda**

**Designer:** This Is Nido (Birmingham, England)

**Web:** www.thisisnido.com

**Vuvav**

**Designer:** Alexander Wende (Ulm, Germany)

**Web:** www.behance.net/alexwende

**Dustin Wilkes**

**Designer:** Kevin Burr (Tennessee, United States)

**Web:** www.ocularink.com

**Camino**

**Designer:** Glen Hobbs/Logoboom (Colorado, United States)

**Twyst**

**Designer:** Gert van Duinen (Emmen, The Netherlands)

**Web:** www.cresk.nl

**Tofu**

**Designer:** Lorena Mirbach (Hamburg, Germany)

**INVIZIO**

handglob

**Invizio**

**Designer:** This Is Nido (Birmingham, England)

**Web:** www.thisisnido.com

**handglob**

**Designer:** FX3/Julien Gionis (Athens, Greece)

**Web:** www.fx3.gr

**Pixelcraft**

**Designer:** Pixelcraft (Dublin, Ireland)

**Web:** www.pixelcraft.ie

**For You!**

**Designer:** Sergey Shapiro (Moscow, Russia)

**Web:** www.fromtheska.ru

**Sotra**

**Designer:** Lukasz Ruszel (Grabownica, Poland)

**Web:** www.midgar.eu

**March**

**Designer:** Me and Mister Jones (Antwerp, Belgium)

**Web:** www.meandmisterjones.com

# DANZK

**Danzk**

**Designer:** Pete Lacey (Frederiksberg, Denmark)

**Web:** www.chopeh.com

**Avenue One**

**Designer:** Mike Rock (Dubai, United Arab Emirates)

**Web:** www.mikerock.co

223

**Facchinelo**

**Designer:** Mads Burcharth (Odense, Denmark)

**Web:** www.mabu.dk

**Arc Al Rajhi Cement**

**Designer:** Ghiath Lahham (Dubai, United Arab Emirates)

**Web:** www.ghiathlahham.com

Rikke Kristine

CRISLABNO

**Rikke Kristine**

**Designer:** Pete Lacey (Frederiksberg, Denmark)

**Web:** www.chopeh.com

**Cris Labno**

**Designer:** Cris Labno (Krakow, Poland)

**Web:** www.crislabno.com

time bomb

**Unreel Fishwear**

**Designer:** Mike Erickson (California, United States)

**Web:** www.logomotive.net

**Time Bomb**

**Designer:** Lorena Mirbach (Hamburg, Germany)

**Stir**

**Designer:** Megan Kirby/The Washington Athletic Club (Washington, United States)

**Web:** www.megankirbydesign.com

**Femina**

**Designer:** Sergey Babenko (Kiev, Ukraine)

225

**Al Manzil Hotel**

**Designer:** Ghiath Lahham (Dubai, United Arab Emirates)

**Web:** www.ghiathlahham.com

**Peppe**

**Designer:** Saawan Ebe (Andhra Pradesh, India)

**Web:** www.studiosaawan.com

**Fogra**

**Designer:** Sean O'Grady (County Mayo, Ireland)

**Web:** www.fogradesign.com

**Sa Scène**

**Designer:** Nadim Twal (London, England)

**Alyasra**

**Designer:** Ghiath Lahham (Dubai, United Arab Emirates)

**Web:** www.ghiathlahham.com

**FiftyFifty**

**Designer:** JamFactory (Bristol, England)

**Web:** www.jam-factory.com

**Niven Landscaping**

**Designer:** Josh Hayes (Victoria, Australia)

**Web:** www.hayesimage.com.au

**Gotovim.ru**

**Designer:** Denis Olenik (Minsk, Belarus)

**Web:** www.denisolenik.com

227

Jacobs & Sons Carrots

**Anna Lord's**

**Designer:** The Logo Factory (Ontario, Canada)

**Web:** www.thelogofactory.com

**Jacobs & Sons Carrots**

**Designer:** Josh Hayes (Victoria, Australia)

**Web:** www.hayesimage.com.au

ARCUS
CONSULTING

**Rockin'**

**Designer:** José De Wal (Winschoten, The Netherlands)

**Web:** www.josedesign.nl

**Arcus Consulting**

**Designer:** Anthony Lane (Minnesota, United States)

**Web:** www.012485.com

**Bird**

**Designer:** Peter Vasvari (Karokatona, Hungary)

**Web:** www.petervasvari.com

**Avenude**

**Designer:** Gert van Duinen (Emmen, The Netherlands)

**Web:** www.cresk.nl

**Pencil**

**Designer:** Reghardt Grobbelaar (Pretoria, South Africa)

**Web:** www.reghardt.com

**Chain Gang**

**Designer:** Lorena Mirbach (Germany)

229

**Saawan**

**Designer:** Saawan Ebe (Andhra Pradesh, India)

**Web:** www.studiosaawan.com

**Mono Software**

**Designer:** Mike Erickson (California, United States)

**Web:** www.logomotive.net

**Jive**

**Designer:** Raja Sandhu (Ontario, Canada)

**Web:** www.rajasandhu.com

**Oasis**

**Designer:** Lorena Mirbach (Germany)

**Jesters**

**Designer:** Mike Erickson (California, United States)

**Web:** www.logomotive.net

**Tarfir**

**Designer:** Cris Labno (Krakow, Poland)

**Web:** www.crislabno.com

**BR&ING**

**Designer:** Gareth Hardy (Birmingham, England)

**Web:** www.downwithdesign.com

**Libera**

**Designer:** Alexander Badovksy (Kiev, Ukraine)

**Web:** www.badovsky.com

# 18

# INITIALS AND MONOGRAMS

THIS CHAPTER SHOWCASES logos that feature the use of alphabetic characters to form a mark. Initials often stand for the name of the entity that the logo identifies and can be one letterform or more. A monogram is a combination of letterform or letterforms that overlap or are an amalgamation to form one graphical focal point. Initials and monograms help the viewer to remember the name of a brand, organization, or individual.

**Deep Guy**

**Designer:** Muhammad Ali Effendy (Sindh, Pakistan)

**Pakuy**

**Designer:** Muamer Adilovic (Sarajevo, Bosnia, and Herzegovina)

**Web:** www.muameradilovic.com

**Aaron Storry**

**Designer:** Pete Lacey (Frederiksberg, Denmark)

**Web:** www.chopeh.com

**RealtyWeb**

**Designer:** Alexander Wende (Ulm, Germany)

**Web:** www.behance.net/alexwende

**Ça Roule**

**Designer:** Roy Smith (Norwich, England)

**Web:** www.roysmithdesign.com

**ADM**

**Designer:** Me and Mister Jones (Antwerp, Belgium)

**Web:** www.meandmisterjones.com

**Rypar**

**Designer:** Jan Zabransky (Zlin, Czech Republic)

**Web:** www.janzabransky.cz

**Musicmaster**

**Designer:** Mike Rock (Dubai, United Arab Emirates)

**Web:** www.mikerock.co

**The Organic Feed Company**

**Designer:** Roy Smith (Norwich, England)

**Web:** www.roysmithdesign.com

236

**Security 4 Transit**

**Designer:** Koodoz Design (Victoria, Australia)

**Web:** www.koodoz.com.au

**Anthony Lane**

**Designer:** Anthony Lane (Minnesota, United States)

**Web:** www.012485.com

**Ross Poultry**

**Designer:** Roy Smith (Norwich, England)

**Web:** www.roysmithdesign.com

**Moving Box**

**Designer:** Anthony Lane (Minnesota, United States)

**Web:** www.012485.com

**Costa Macaroni**

**Designer:** Leighton Hubbell (California, United States)

**Web:** www.leightonhubbell.com

237

**SlickPixel**

**Designer:** 903 Creative (Virginia, United States)

**Web:** www.903creative.com

**Robin Bond**

**Designer:** José De Wal (Winschoten, The Netherlands)

**Web:** www.josedesign.nl

**Antoine Antoniadis**

**Designer:** FX3/Julien Gionis (Athens, Greece)

**Web:** www.fx3.gr

**Filmhouse**

**Designer:** Muamer Adilovic (Sarajevo, Bosnia, and Herzegovina)

**Web:** www.muameradilovic.com

**Ximo**

**Designer:** Gareth Hardy (Birmingham, England)

**Web:** www.downwithdesign.com

**West Austin Properties**

**Designer:** Burn Creative (Pennsylvania, United States)

**Web:** www.burncreative.com

**Flight Imports**

**Designer:** Carrihan Creative Group/ Christopher Hanley (Texas, United States)

**Web:** www.carrihan.com

**Heritage Retirement Advisors**

**Designer:** Glen Hobbs/Logoboom (Colorado, United States)

**Wiley**

**Designer:** Gerard Huerta (Connecticut, United States)

**Art Directors:** Craig Bernhardt, Janice Fudyma

**Web:** www.gerardhuerta.com

**Robert Busch School of Design**

**Designer:** Rich Arnold (New York, United States)

**Web:** www.deadeyedesignny.com

240

**GBG**

**Designer:** Lukasz Ruszel (Grabownica, Poland)

**Web:** www.midgar.eu

**Dercums Research**

**Designer:** Carrihan Creative Group/ Christopher Hanley (Texas, United States)

**Web:** www.carrihan.com

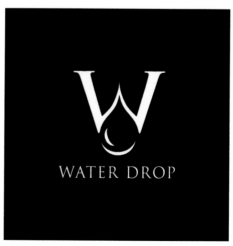

**Reputeer**

**Designer:** Rich Scott (Queensland, Australia)

**Web:** www.designabot.net

**Water Drop**

**Designer:** Peter Vasvari (Karokatona, Hungary)

**Web:** www.petervasvari.com

**Luuk Hartsema**

**Designer:** Euan MacKenzie (East Kilbride, Scotland)

**Web:** www.euanmackenzie.com

**Quail**

**Designer:** John Neiner (Massachusetts, United States)

**Web:** www.neinercreative.com

241

**Money Saving Tactics**

**Designer:** Reghardt Grobbelaar (Pretoria, South Africa)

**Web:** www.reghardt.com

**Noah Borer Video Productions**

**Designer:** Muhammad Ali Effendy (Sindh, Pakistan)

**Kallaway**

**Designer:** Roy Smith (Norwich, England)

**Web:** www.roysmithdesign.com

**903 Creative**

**Designer:** 903 Creative (Virginia, United States)

**Web:** www.903creative.com

**Spelling Entertainment, Inc.**

**Designer:** Gerard Huerta (Connecticut, United States)

**Art Director:** Jon Ferrari

**Web:** www.gerardhuerta.com

**Nice Typography**

**Designer:** Stan Grinapol (New York, United States)

**Web:** www.scribbleandtweak.com

**Solangel Properties**

**Designer:** Gareth Hardy (Birmingham, England)

**Web:** www.downwithdesign.com

**Electric Lemonade**

**Designer:** The Logo Factory (Ontario, Canada)

**Web:** www.thelogofactory.com

243

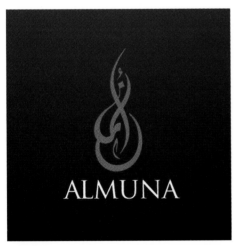

**Almuna**

**Designer:** Nadim Twal (London, England)

**HBO**

**Designer:** Gerard Huerta (Connecticut, United States)

**Web:** www.gerardhuerta.com

**Royalty Records Management**

**Designer:** Sergey Babenko (Kiev, Ukraine)

**Michael Spitz**

**Designer:** Michael Spitz (Philadelphia, United States)

**Web:** www.michaelspitz.com

**Relentless Insignia**

**Designer:** Studio_Fla (London, England)

**Web:** www.studiofla.com

**Airpoint Amsterdam**

**Designer:** José De Wal (Winschoten, The Netherlands)

**Web:** www.josedesign.nl

**Made By Thomas**

**Designer:** Made By Thomas (Vlaanderen, Belgium)

**Web:** www.madebythomas.com

**Lindsay Quinn**

**Designer:** Anthony Lane (Minnesota, United States)

**Web:** www.012485.com

**Mister**

**Designer:** Mister (Glasgow, Scotland)

**Web:** www.studiomister.com

**Elprom**

**Designer:** Lukasz Ruszel (Grabownica, Poland)

**Web:** www.midgar.eu

**Flirt Salon**

**Designer:** Carrihan Creative Group/
Christopher Hanley (Texas, United States)

**Web:** www.carrihan.com

**Dianne Dieplo**

**Designer:** Gareth Hardy (Birmingham,
England)

**Web:** www.downwithdesign.com

**Kaimere**

**Designer:** Mike Rock (Dubai, United Arab
Emirates)

**Web:** www.mikerock.co

**One**

**Designer:** Mike Rock (Dubai, United Arab
Emirates)

**Web:** www.mikerock.co

**Hanuet Wine**

**Designer:** Euan MacKenzie (East Kilbride, Scotland)

**Web:** www.euanmackenzie.com

**Pistilli Realty Group**

**Designer:** Wizemark (Backa Palanka, Serbia)

**Web:** www.wizemark.com

247

**John Lauren**

**Designer:** Andrej Matic (Belgrade, Serbia)

**Web:** www.logohype.net

**Ezop**

**Designer:** Jan Zabransky (Zlin, Czech Republic)

**Web:** www.janzabransky.cz

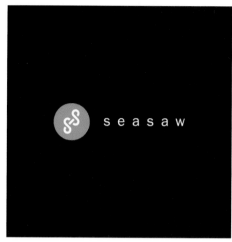

**248**

**Blue Rose Wealth Management**

**Designer:** Wizemark (Backa Palanka, Serbia)

**Web:** www.wizemark.com

**Seasaw**

**Designer:** Wizemark (Backa Palanka, Serbia)

**Web:** www.wizemark.com

**Central Eyeworks**

**Designer:** Leighton Hubbell (California, United States)

**Web:** www.leightonhubbell.com

**Athens Partners Investments**

**Designer:** Carrihan Creative Group/ Christopher Hanley (Texas, United States)

**Web:** www.carrihan.com

**Finishing Touch**

**Designer:** Brandsimplicity (Maddington, Australia)

**Web:** www.brandsimplicity.com.au

**Marie Beetge**

**Designer:** Marie Beetge (Cape Town, South Africa)

**Web:** www.mariebeetge.com

249

**Toy Gun Films**

**Designer:** Foundry Co (Oklahoma, United States)

**Web:** www.foundrycollective.com

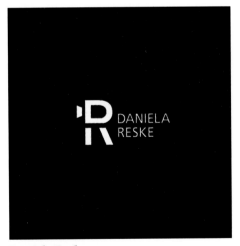

**Daniela Reske**

**Designer:** Alexander Wende (Ulm, Germany)

**Web:** www.behance.net/alexwende

**Rubloff**

**Designer:** Mike Erickson (California, United States)

**Web:** www.logomotive.net

**Vectory Belle**

**Designer:** Vanja Bjallic (Split, Croatia)

**Web:** www.vectorybelle.da portfolio.com

**Theo's Cycle Shop**

**Designer:** Gareth Hardy (Birmingham, England)

**Web:** www.downwithdesign.com

# 19

# EMBLEMS AND CHARACTERS

THE FINAL CHAPTER of the showcase section presents emblems or logos featuring illustrated characters. Emblems are sometimes confused with wordmarks because they sometimes include a word or series of words, but they're enclosed in or surrounded by an assisting shape. Emblems also may include pictorial elements, including illustrated characters.

**Avenue Coffee**

**Designer:** Wizemark (Backa Palanka, Serbia)

**Web:** www.wizemark.com

**Hoppenia Wild Games**

**Designer:** Sergey Babenko (Kiev, Ukraine)

**Lee Jackson**

**Designer:** Roy Smith (Norwich, England)

**Web:** www.roysmithdesign.com

**The Nelson**

**Designer:** Wizemark (Backa Palanka, Serbia)

**Web:** www.wizemark.com

**See:evil**

**Designer:** Gareth Hardy (Birmingham, England)

**Web:** www.downwithdesign.com

**Ember**

**Designer:** JamFactory (Bristol, England)

**Web:** www.jam-factory.com

**Chicken Hut**

**Designer:** Oronoz Brandesign (Chihuahua, Mexico)

**Web:** www.alanoronoz.com

**Deep Ellum Brewing Company**

**Designer:** Carrihan Creative Group/ Christopher Hanley (Texas, United States)

**Web:** www.carrihan.com

**Private Grave**

**Designer:** Dan Gretta (Pennsylvania, United States)

**Web:** www.dannygretta.com

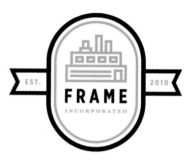

**Frame Incorporated**

**Designer:** Tim Boelaars (Amsterdam, The Netherlands)

**Web:** www.timboelaars.nl

**S.H. United**

**Designer:** 903 Creative (Virginia, United States)

**Web:** www.903creative.com

**Down With Design**

**Designer:** Gareth Hardy (Birmingham, England)

**Web:** www.downwithdesign.com

**Green Monkey Tea**

**Designer:** James Strange (Nebraska, United States)

**Cookie Autobot**

**Designer:** James Strange (Nebraska, United States)

**Black Coffee**

**Designer:** Dan Gretta (Pennsylvania, United States)

**Web:** www.dannygretta.com

**Viral Ad Network**

**Designer:** JamFactory (Bristol, England)

**Web:** www.jam-factory.com

**Paymo**

**Designer:** Andrei Gadoiu (Bihor, Romania)

**Web:** www.fivetailors.com

**Dodge's**

**Designer:** Randy Heil (Arizona, United States)

**Web:** www.randyheil.com

**MSDN TV**

**Designer:** Turbomilk LTD (Samara, Russia)

**Web:** www.turbomilk.com

**Kyle's Kayaking Safaris**

**Designer:** John Boerckel (Pennsylvania, United States)

**Web:** www.johnboerckel.com

**Shirokuma, Inc.**

**Designer:** The Logo Factory (Ontario, Canada)

**Web:** www.thelogofactory.com

**Macafe Marketing**

**Designer:** Ivan Bobrov (Novosibirsk, Russia)

257

**Blog Blog Black Sheep**

**Designer:** Jerron Ames (Utah, United States)

**3 Vines**

**Designer:** Leighton Hubbell (California, United States)

**Web:** www.leightonhubbell.com

**Peace Love & Understanding**

**Designer:** Attak ('s-Hertegosenbasch, The Netherlands)

**Web:** www.attakweb.com

**Taca**

**Designer:** Niall Staines (Dublin, Ireland)

**Web:** www.niallstaines.com

**Debut London**

**Designer:** Michael Spitz (Pennsylvania, United States)

**Web:** www.michaelspitz.com

**Sweet Land Confectionary**

**Designer:** Oronoz Brandesign (Chihuahua, Mexico)

**Web:** www.alanoronoz.com

**Chopeh**

**Designer:** Pete Lacey (Frederiksberg, Denmark)

**Web:** www.chopeh.com

**The Olde World Rug Washing Company**

**Designer:** Jerron Ames (Utah, United States)

259

**Bendigo Community Farmers Market**

**Designer:** Studio Ink (Victoria, Australia)

**Web:** www.studioink.com.au

**The Rutland Arms Hotel**

**Designer:** Roy Smith (Norwich, England)

**Web:** www.roysmithdesign.com

**The Bean**

**Designer:** The Logo Factory (Ontario, Canada)

**Web:** www.thelogofactory.com

**Wyldlyfe**

**Designer:** Dan Gretta (Pennsylvania, United States)

**Web:** www.dannygretta.com

**Quad City Mallards**

**Designer:** Matt Kauzlarich (Michigan, United States)

**La Bella**

**Designer:** Studio Ink (Victoria, Australia)

**Web:** www.studioink.com.au

**The Lost Chambers Atlantis**

**Designer:** Ghiath Lahham (Dubai, United Arab Emirates)

**Web:** www.ghiathlahham.com

**Stems & Petals**

**Designer:** Mel Campbell (California, United States)

**Web:** www.six17.net

**Food Fossickers**

**Designer:** Studio Ink (Victoria, Australia)

**Web:** www.studioink.com.au

**Green Path Garden Supply**

**Designer:** Jerron Ames (Utah, United States)

**Amsterdam United**

**Designer:** Tim Boelaars (Amsterdam, The Netherlands)

**Web:** www.timboelaars.nl

**Wharton Wildmen**

**Designer:** Matt Kauzlarich (Michigan, United States)

**The Serious Sausage Co!**

**Designer:** Sneh Roy (Sydney, Australia)

**Web:** www.littleboxofideas.com

**dotmonster**

**Designer:** Type08 (Koprivnica, Croatia)

**Web:** www.type08.com

**Cards For Care**

**Designer:** Michael Spitz (Pennsylvania, United States)

**Web:** www.michaelspitz.com

**Men Cook Now**

**Designer:** Jerron Ames (Utah, United States)

263

**Rail Head BBQ**

**Designer:** Foundry Co (Oklahoma, United States)

**Web:** www.foundrycollective.com

**Lincoln Classic Bikes**

**Designer:** James Strange (Nebraska, United States)

**Argyll Forest Products**

**Designer:** Euan MacKenzie (East Kilbride, Scotland)

**Web:** www.euanmackenzie.com

**Limerickclasses.com**

**Designer:** Turbomilk LTD (Samara, Russia)

**Web:** www.turbomilk.com

**12 Blues**

**Designer:** Mike Rock (Dubai, United Arab Emirates)

**Web:** www.mikerock.co

**RockSampler**

**Designer:** Oronoz Brandesign (Chihuahua, Mexico)

**Web:** www.alanoronoz.com

**Iconfinder**

**Designer:** Turbomilk LTD (Samara, Russia)

**Web:** www.turbomilk.com

**The Trails**

**Designer:** Foundry Co (Oklahoma, United States)

**Web:** www.foundrycollective.com

**McFly Originals**

**Designer:** Koodoz Design (Victoria, Australia)

**Web:** www.koodoz.com.au

**Godzillas Paintball Team**

**Designer:** Sergey Babenko (Kiev, Ukraine)

**Hegel Toys**

**Designer:** Reghardt Grobbelaar (Pretoria, South Africa)

**Web:** www.reghardt.com

**Carakale**

**Designer:** Nadim Twal (London, England)

**Bottom Feeders Clam Bar**

**Designer:** The Logo Factory (Ontario, Canada)

**Web:** www.thelogofactory.com

**The Loaded Diaper**

**Designer:** Josiah Jost (Alberta, Canada)

**Web:** www.siahdesign.com

**Bath Guardian**

**Designer:** The Logo Factory (Ontario, Canada)

**Web:** www.thelogofactory.com

**Confidently Cruising**

**Designer:** Dan Gretta (Pennsylvania, United States)

**Web:** www.dannygretta.com

267

**Rocket Coffee**

**Designer:** James Strange (Nebraska, United States)

**Zombie Mixer**

**Designer:** James Strange (Nebraska, United States)

**Lionstone**

**Designer:** Mike Rock (Dubai, United Arab Emirates)

**Web:** www.mikerock.co

**A Little FX**

**Designer:** Gareth Hardy (Birmingham, England)

**Web:** www.downwithdesign.com

**California Cajun Foods**

**Designer:** Jerron Ames (Utah, United States)

**Bakken Bears**

**Designer:** Matt Kauzlarich (Michigan, United States)

**Bright Sparks**

**Designer:** Gareth Hardy (Birmingham, England)

**Web:** www.downwithdesign.com

**Lions & Lambs Media Group, LLC**

**Designer:** Gareth Hardy (Birmingham, England)

**Web:** www.downwithdesign.com

**Your Home Theater**

**Designer:** Carrihan Creative Group/ Christopher Hanley (Texas, United States)

**Web:** www.carrihan.com

**Big Game Dinner**

**Designer:** Mackey Saturday (Colorado, United States)

**Web:** www.mackeysaturday.com

Gnomeangel

**Gnomeangel**

**Designer:** Gareth Hardy (Birmingham, England)

**Web:** www.downwithdesign.com

**Raffles Hotels & Resorts**

**Designer:** Me and Mister Jones (Antwerp, Belgium)

**Web:** www.meandmisterjones.com

**Horsens Pirates**

**Designer:** Matt Kauzlarich (Michigan, United States)

**Web:** www.mackeysaturday.com

# STEP INSIDE THE WORLD OF LOGO DESIGN

MANY MOONS AGO, when a lens flare was still a twinkle in Adobe's eye, logos existed. There was no software to help or confuse a designer—just pure creativity using traditional tools. Over time, logo design has evolved, but the function of the logo has remained the same.

Logo design is changing so quickly that what was once viewed as a single element of graphic design is now recognized as its own separate industry and profession. These changes have meant that the people who design logos have had to modify their design behaviors to keep up with the evolution.

In this appendix, I fill you in on the people who create the beloved logos you see every day. You'll gain an understanding of just how far the industry has come since the inception of graphic design as a recognized profession. You'll hear from a variety of designers about their thoughts on the industry today and where it's headed.

## TECHNOLOGY

The real roots of logo design technology are as simple as the human mind and a pencil, which are, of course, still used today. The only real difference between the first designers who picked up their pencils and the present-day industry is the introduction of the computer.

Leighton Hubbell (www.leightonhubbell.com), an award-winning logo designer from Southern California, has been designing logos since the late 1980s. He shared with me his view on how computers have become an essential part of the everyday life of a professional designer:

> *Many significant changes have taken place in the design industry since I got my first job in 1987. When I started out, the use of the computer hadn't really taken hold yet. In contrast, a good number of my colleagues now have never known design without a computer—and some, the Internet.*

There are arguments both for and against computers in the use of design, with some designers claiming that it stifles creativity and goes against some of the fundamental principles of design. Yet there is no denying that the computer has made the process ten times quicker. Computer software plays a pivotal role in logo design today, especially in the way in which a logo is reproduced. It is now impossible to design a logo effectively without the computer.

### SOFTWARE

Regardless of which computer software you use, there seems to be a new update every year—it can be difficult to keep up. The good news is that you don't need the latest software in order to create a functional and successful logo. As long as the software you use is able to output vector graphics, that's all that matters.

Steve Douglas, founder of The Logo Factory (www.thelogofactory.com), a graphic design company based in Ontario, Canada, has a wealth of experience in the art of designing logos. I asked him how the tools he uses to create logos have changed since he first got into the profession:

> *When I first started professionally, back in the early '80s, we didn't have access to computers and desktop publishing technology. My trained "skills" were in the use of Rubylith, Bainbridge board, Letraset, stat camera, galley type, ruling, and technical pens. When I entered the workforce as a junior graphic designer in 1980 (even back then there were very few full-time gigs for illustrators), desktop computers and desktop publishing were pretty well science fiction. Everything was done by hand on acetate overlays. My first exposure to computer illustration and design was at home through the old Amiga platform in the mid-'80s.*
>
> *I remember there were two "professional-level" design programs for the Amiga—Pro Draw (pretty well a poor man's Illustrator) and Pro Page (similar to a very basic version of Quark)—and tooling around with them allowed me to understand the technical side of things. Fairly rudimentary stuff—came with only three fonts—but*

*the basic principles (Bezier curves, kerning, and so on) still applied. I had a LaserJet printer that needed a PostScript interpreter cartridge to print anything, and downloading to the printer often took an hour per page. At the time, it was state of the art. I remember telling my old boss that desktop publishing was going to change the way design was done. He laughed at me, telling me that computers were a passing fad.*

*That's how many people looked upon computers as creative tools back in the day, so most "training" consisted of learning how to do things by yourself. I used the Amiga loyally until about '95 when it blew up, and I had to borrow money from my parents to buy a Macintosh. My first was a 6100/66 (the 66 referred to 66 megahertz processing power) and I had to borrow Photoshop and Illustrator from friends. In those days, Photoshop took about five minutes to fire up, there were no layers, and there was only one level of Undo. I stayed on top of the technology by reading books (the Internet wasn't really in wide use) and by practicing. Lots of practice. I considered going back to night school for some courses, but I seemed to adapt fairly quickly, so I never bothered. Do I miss the old techniques? Sure. There was a certain amount of skill that was lost when the design industry moved from analog to digital.*

Mike Erickson, of Logomotive Designs (www.logomotive.net), based in Roseville, California, believes that although the advancement of technology has helped, it hasn't changed the fundamental practices of designing a logo:

*You can easily design a logo with tools as simple as a pencil or crayon. Of course, you would have to turn it into a digital file, but the bottom line is, you're using the same tools. The effects in the software are the only things that really change the technology. Everything else remains unchanged. The vector formats, Bezier curves, color fills, and so on—they remain consistent. I'd rather use the same old pencil or program that gets the job done.*

This isn't to say that software is evil and should be discredited. Software has played an integral role in streamlining the workflow of logo designers. Luckily, designers have had multiple options as technology has evolved:

- **Adobe Illustrator:** Adobe Illustrator is perhaps the most well-known vector graphics program due to the massive popularity of the Adobe Creative Suite. It was originally developed by Apple way back in 1986 when vector-ready software was still in its infancy. Having gone through more than 20 updated versions of the original package, Illustrator is now one of the established options on the market.
- **Macromedia Freehand:** Some experienced designers still prefer to use Macromedia freehand, which is very similar in the functionality of Macromedia. No updates for Freehand have been provided since 2007, and none are planned as of this writing.
- **CorelDRAW:** Released three years after Illustrator, CorelDRAW was provided as part of Corel's desktop publishing suite. Corel was the first vector software that I purchased in 1995, and it has come a long way since, with the program now in its 14th release.
- **Inkscape:** Inkscape is a freeware application, available to everyone free of charge. As result, it's becoming a more popular option for new designers.

## DOES THIS MEAN THE DEATH OF THE PENCIL?

With software being such an increasingly important part of the process, this question is a logical one. I've spoken to some designers who carry out the complete logo design process on-screen, bypassing the option for sketching using traditional media altogether.

Mike Erickson believes that the easy access to computers often leads to overuse and a premature reliability on the machine to do all the work for you:

> *The younger generation has been brought up with computers as part of their everyday environment, so when it comes to design, they rely on the computer to do everything for them. In the old days, we did everything with the pencil and ink. All the artwork had to be camera-ready, but it's a lot different now—everything is digital. The pencil is mightier than the mouse.*

Ultimately, it would be foolish to think that the art of drawing would become completely extinct, but it's partly dependent on the education that new designers receive and any bad habits they may have picked up. You can easily design a logo without having to draw on paper, but I think that this opportunity for traditional artistic expression can only help to broaden a designer's skill set, not to mention his or her mind.

## DESIGN EDUCATION

274

One of the biggest debates within the design industry surrounds whether it is essential to have an official education in design to become a successful designer. Although design does have its theories, I believe that talent is a natural gift that can't be taught—it *can* be encouraged and honed, though.

Steve Douglas thinks that a formal education can help, but it doesn't necessarily guarantee a successful career:

> *A design education is certainly helpful, as long as it's a decent design education. I've interviewed college graduates for positions at my shop, and many don't have the necessary skills to work in a fast-paced environment. It's not their fault—when I do hire them, they learn pretty quickly "in the trenches." When I was an art student, things like Illustrator and Photoshop were unheard of. As far as my education goes, I attended illustration in college, but it was so long ago that any current skills—desktop software and what have you—are pretty well self-taught. That's true today as well—the technology is advancing so fast that it's difficult to keep courses current. Of course, there are the old standbys—life drawing, design, and color theory. Those remain valuable to any designer and an important part of any education.*

Glen Hobbs, who designs logos on a freelance basis in Colorado, understands that a design education can come in many forms and doesn't always have to be undertaken at a recognized education facility:

*An "education" is essential, to be sure. But exactly what form that education comes in can vary, I think. Case in point: I have a degree in visual communications from a technical branch of a major university. The curriculum was developed and taught by industry professionals. It was a great foundation to get me in the door for an entry-level position oh so many years ago (where the learning really starts). My brother, however, also an accomplished designer, did not go to school for it. Rather, he worked under the tutelage of professionals who recognized his natural talents and gave him opportunity to grow.*

*So where does that leave us? Well, I think that the most important thing for any designer is a thirst for knowledge. And not just about our chosen profession. The more we open ourselves up, the more we explore; the more we are aware of the world around us and how it works (or not), then the better we are at creating visual communication that is relevant in that world. A formal education in design is a solid beginning. I just think the key is to realize that formal education is just that—only the beginning.*

Kevin Burr, of Ocular Ink (`www.ocularink.com`), based in Nashville, Tennessee, recognizes that his design education experience has benefited him as a designer and helped him to pinpoint his preferred occupation:

*I received my bachelor's degree in design communications upon graduating from Belmont University in 2004. For me, an education in design was essential. While at Belmont, Professor Dan Johnson noticed my love for logo and identity design. He saw my interest early on as a freshman and made it a focus most of my time at school. Upon graduating, it seemed natural to promote myself as a logo and identity designer.*

*The college experience gives you time to hone your skills and begin the process of creating a portfolio. Having the extra eyes on your work also allows you to learn how to accept criticism and gives your peers the opportunity to offer an outside opinion of your work. This is a huge part of developing your skills as a designer. Let's face it—we all have big egos. It's a good thing to have your ego beaten down every now and then. This helps you grow as a designer. Having a handful of professors at your fingertips to answer your questions doesn't hurt either.*

Rather than just seek the opinion of designers who are already working professionally, I felt it was important to gain the thoughts of students hoping to secure design jobs in the future. I spoke to Stephanie Reeves, a final-year student at Birmingham City University in the United Kingdom, studying visual communication. I asked her if she was worried about her prospects once she graduates:

*I don't think worried is the word—more petrified. There is a lot of student work in magazines and on the web that is beautiful, professional, and finished to such a standard that makes my head fall to the desk. There are always going to be people better than you, and I often feel that if I don't get that all-important job straight after I finish my education, then that's it, I'm a has-been. Also, at 23, I can sometimes think that I'll be too old for that fashionable agency hiring fresh, young graduate blood.*

*Two words that are constantly pushed in front of most undergrads of any degree now are work experience. As good as your tutors are, their teachings are nothing compared to what you'll learn in a professional environment. The long-term placements I've had with agencies and companies means that I already have a workplace history and a professional network. I've worked with the university magazine, in collaborative projects and exhibitions, and entered student awards, too. I'm hoping that so much involvement might give me an advantage over other graduates (and a real workplace has shown me that I'm still very young).*

*My visual communications course is very broad and the students in my class alone are so varied in the paths our work takes that lecturing us all about identity and branding in the same way would prove useless. In some ways, this isn't a bad thing; it's provided a "learn from each other" environment that has allowed us to work in our own ways, backed up all the way through with one-to-one tutorials from tutors. However, at the same time, I think it's not left us with much technical background on the finer points of the "art of a logo," for example.*

*However much industry experience your tutor brings to the class, though, and however much confidence he or she gives you that your work is up to standard, you'll never really have the confidence you get from a real client saying "yes" to their new identity. The course gave me the confidence to approach companies for work experience, and that work experience has given me the confidence to take on the freelance jobs I'm now getting.*

Nathan Sarlow (www.cobaltcow.com), a freelance logo designer in Detroit, Michigan, suggests that the education system could be altered to provide graduates with a greater understanding of the industry that they hope to inhibit in the future:

*It seems that the majority of people who graduate from design school come out with the same knowledge and a similar style. I personally feel that the education part of the design industry needs to be guided more by active designers and less by teachers (who used to be designers). This way, the students would be learning more about current real-world design and not theoretical design that will only give them a false sense of their worth to the industry.*

My own design education is a little different—I didn't study a specific discipline of design, but my education covered almost every aspect of it. This helped me to identify which area of design I wanted to focus on, but I think this broad scope hinders some people's progress. Out of a class of 30, only 4 or 5 of the students went on to hold down employment within the industry.

What does the future hold for education in the field of logo design? We might see specialist courses that focus solely on the art of designing logos. We could even see branding and identity academies or colleges. Education can only be a good thing, but the fact remains that if you have artistic ability, you'll have a great advantage over those who don't.

## Keep learning

The great thing about design is that you never stop learning. Art gives you the opportunity to explore new avenues of creativity with every new project that lands in your lap.

Mike Erickson recognizes that everyone, regardless of individual character and personality, has the capacity to continue learning throughout his or her design career:

*I would say that I'm mostly a self-taught designer but I've always had a natural talent for art. I can remember being in art classes in college, and the instructor would ask me why as I was even in the class because he felt that the standard of the work I was producing was already beyond the teachings of the syllabus. But I was in the class because I feel that you can never stop learning—we learn something new every day, regardless of age or experience.*

Kevin Burr believes that a mixture of both formal education and using his own initiative to learn new skills has helped him to forge a career in designing identities professionally:

*In the grand scheme of things, if it weren't for Belmont and my professor continually motivating me to follow my passion with logo and identity design, my own initiative to learn wouldn't exist. It was there where I learned the fundamentals, which have helped pave the way to learning the intricate details of those fundamentals. I learned that I love logos and identity at school, and that's more important to me than the daily learning I do now.*

I can honestly say that I have learned more about design and, in particular, logo design since I left university than I did during my time in school. That comes down to an awareness that in order to improve you can't just sit and recite the things you already know. There will always be someone out there who is willing to push the boundaries of creativity, and you should be prepared to be that person.

The best form of education is working professionally in your field. You can read all the textbooks under the sun, but until it comes time to put what you know into practice, you won't truly learn any of the tricks of the trade that matter. This applies to any industry, not just design. This is where I believe that designers without a formal education can really shine, because they have no predetermined opinions on how things should be done and can absorb real-world skills.

## THE RISE OF THE WEB

The Internet has changed our lives forever. Whether it will have a positive or negative long-term effect on society remains to be seen, but it has certainly cracked open the world of logo design from the inside.

### INCREASED OPPORTUNITIES

The Internet has, in effect, reduced the size of the design industry—not in terms of numbers, but in terms of how easy it is to make contact with designers and design companies from all over the globe. Never before has it been so easy for a company on one side of the world to request the services of designers who are located thousands of miles away. This would have been impossible as recently as a couple decades ago, unless the designer or firm had a world-renowned reputation.

## THE PRICE WAR

Some designers prefer not to reveal their prices; others have no qualms in doing so. With more competition, particularly for the smaller to midsize projects, price seems to play an ever more prominent role in clients choosing which designer to go with. As the Internet is responsible for broadening the competition of both freelancers and design firms, the prices that they set have had to become equally competitive. As we all know, one of the main ways a potential client will find your work online is through a search engine. Unfortunately, most people seeking a logo will more often than not go for the cheap option. This results in thousands of designers targeting key words relating to low prices. The cheaper the price, the more likely it is that the number of leads will increase.

It's common sense that if your prices are set at rock bottom you'll have to finish many more projects to make the same money you would by charging the rate that your time deserves. When people charge rock-bottom prices, they have to work quickly to make a reasonable living—and the quality of their work suffers.

Sean O'Grady (www.fogradesign.com), a graphic designer from Mayo, Ireland, believes that price is having a significant effect on freelance designers in particular:

> The design industry is now reduced to which designer can offer the lowest price for design work. In fact, I have seen some prospective clients offering only $10 to anyone who can design a logo for their company, or even nothing in some cases to gain a portfolio piece.

In effect, there is nothing you can do about low prices. If there are people out there who are willing to work for next to nothing, let them do it. The clients who they're doing the work for are probably not worth the time and energy anyway.

## SPECULATIVE WORK

Perhaps the biggest concern to designers as a result of the Internet is that it has played an enormous part in the increased participation and awareness of speculative (or spec) work. Spec work is when a client is only willing to pay for a service after they've seen examples of how the end product will look. You may have been asked in the past to provide some sketches to try to "convince" a potential client that you're the right designer for them.

Doing work without getting paid for it doesn't make sense. Unfortunately, many designers are willing to take the risk, because they're blinded by the potential reward.

Glen Hobbs believes that spec work in the long terms has a negative effect on the design industry:

*I found a hilarious spoof post a while back that really summed this up. It was from a designer saying that he was looking for new clients. He asked any company interested in his services to simply mail him a check for what they think is a fair amount. He'd cash all the checks, spend some of the money, and see how it all feels. Then he'd decide whom he wants to work with. Ridiculous? Yes.*

*I don't do spec work. My time is far too valuable to me. It can possibly have some short-term upside (if your spec is chosen), but long term, I think it undermines our industry.*

To further compound the problem, there are now many "crowd-sourcing" websites where spec work is the name of the game. Thousands of designers take part in design contests every day in the hopes of maybe landing some real-world work. Doing spec work is gambling with your time, time that you could be spending working on a portfolio of self-initiated projects that answer design briefs.

## THE FIGHT AGAINST PLAGIARISM

Unfortunately, the Internet has brought with it another problem: With the misconception that they won't be caught due to the size of the web, more and more plagiarists are taking the work of other designers and the logos of existing businesses and passing them off as their own. The plagiarist is either a business owner who is seeking to get a logo on the cheap or another designer aiming to create a fake portfolio to try to lure unsuspecting potential clients into hiring him. Finding out that someone else is unlawfully using your logo is a tiring situation to be involved in, for both the designer and the client.

279

Most people seem to think that it's perfectly acceptable to take any image that has been published online and start using it in any way that they please. With more instances of logo copyright infringement becoming more common, it seems that there is no way to solve this problem. As long as there are people willing to steal existing works, designers will be susceptible to becoming a victim of plagiarism.

## WHAT CAME FIRST: THE LOGO OR THE NAME?

A new technique, developed mainly through the advancement of the Internet, is to do the whole process backward. Some websites have appeared that allow startups to buy brand names coupled with an identity off the shelf, ready-made, sitting in wait for a potential owner. A new business owner might see a logo/name and think, "That's perfect for me—I'll take it!" They buy the logo, download the necessary files, and go on their way, slapping the logo on everything they cast their eyes upon. It's essentially a happy ending. Or is it?

Let's set another scenario: You're getting married and you need a wedding cake made. You want it to fit into the theme of your wedding and look exactly how you want. Where would you go to get such a fantastic cake? Would you go to the local bakery and pick a cheap cake that had been sitting in the shop window for days, or would you contact a specialist who will listen to your requirements, suggest the best solution based on your needs, and create a custom-designed cake that achieves everything you ever dreamed of? If you're serious about your wedding, the custom-designed route is the likely choice.

The danger of buying a ready-made brand is that there is no communication between the designer and the client *before* a solution is created. Communication is key during the branding process and removing the design brief stage is dangerous.

Most ready-made brands are nothing more than a named logo (if you can even call it a logo—it doesn't identify anything until it's purchased). An image is created and a name is slapped onto it: ChickenEgg! BatFish! Would any professional business really use a brand name like that? There have been numerous cases of ready-made logos being direct copies of existing logos or at the very least heavily inspired by them. ***Remember:*** A successful and effective logo or brand should be unique.

Leighton Hubbell discusses why the premise of selling stock logos and identities have hooked some people:

> *I can understand why people gave it a try. Some of them were established designers needing to pay some bills, and a few of them were amateurs trying to break into the business. But they are missing the single most important point about logo design: It's not a "one-size-fits-all" type of medium. A logo design is custom-tailored for each client and their specific needs and goals. What works perfectly for one business or service won't necessarily work for another. It is not a beauty contest. It is not a commodity item. It is not stock.*

> *Like any logo designer, I have lots of logo concepts that haven't been used. For every logo that gets approved, there are dozens that may never see the light of day. Unfortunately, that's a common side effect of our profession. Another is that the design that gets approved isn't always the strongest piece. On the positive side, if a logo doesn't get selected, it can always have a home in your portfolio.*

> *Part of being a creative person is showing others what you are capable of. And some designers figured that if they can't be used by that client, then there's surely got to be a client or business out there who will want to use my super-cool logo concept for something! You could save it on the hard drive and retool it for another client (which is usually the case), or you could try to sell it on the open market.*

> *Innocently enough, there is some validity to that idea. And with an ever-growing stockpile of work adding up every week and the economy being what it is, the idea came up to try to sell these designs online for some "easy" money. No harm, no foul. Or so it seemed.*

> *With business being even slower for a good portion of the logo design community, there seemed to be a major surge to keep up with the Joneses and fatten the online portfolio with hypothetical and contrived logo designs, just waiting for the customers to come along. And this doesn't even cover the logo contest sites.*

> *Now, don't get me wrong—there will always be work that you create to expand and improve your portfolio, and I am no different. Maybe it was a project a client never finished. Or a cool movie or TV show inspired you. There's nothing wrong with that. I am always working on my book.*

The worrying fact is that some designers, especially those new to the industry, think that the only way to get established and build a portfolio of work (and also to make some quick cash) is to get involved with the creation of stock identities. I think that the massive influx of fake logos in the portfolios of beginning to intermediate designers is due to a number of factors:

- Misperceived tactics of how to build a reputation
- Lack of education on how to answer a real brief
- Fewer opportunities, leading to fake logos as being a marketing tactic

## PROMOTION

With the numbers of professional designers increasing every day, it's more important than ever to promote yourself in order to remain competitive. Luckily, an abundance of methods and mediums are available to allow you to communicate with potential clients—locally or around the world—to let them know what you offer.

### PUTTING TOGETHER A PORTFOLIO

Ultimately, the portfolio is the most important tool in promoting the skill set and experience of any designer, regardless of the field in which her or she operates.

How much work should you show in your portfolio? Should you show everything that you've ever done? The simple answer is that you should show only the work that you feel will help you to land future projects and impress potential new employers. If you put effort and thought into each project that you undertake, you'll be able to show everything you've ever designed.

### COVERING ALL THE BASES

The Internet has opened up avenues for designers to be able to upload work to various portfolio portals, which increases the chances of individual recognition from both peers and potential clients.

Leighton Hubbell, who has been working in the industry for over 20 years, has had to adapt his promotional tactics in order to keep up with the influx of competition:

> *For years, the guide to self-promotion was fairly traditional. You made contacts through getting work in front of key individuals, whether it was sending out promotional pieces through the mail, dropping samples off at a local agency or business, or just making cold calls. You did just about anything you could to get your portfolio in front of someone. Every once in a while, you made a contact through somebody you knew. Slowly, you built yourself a reputation—first locally, then regionally, and so on. I managed to make a pretty good living getting business that way, until a few years ago when everything changed.*

> *The single most important change is visibility and making the most of it. It used to be enough to just have a website. Now, you need a web presence. There is so much competition out there (some good and some not so good) that designers really need*

*to show what they can do and set themselves apart from everyone else. In this*
*business, you need to adapt or you can get left behind very quickly.*

My own promotional tactics have led me to understand that this is a predominantly digital world. Just having a portfolio that you can touch by hand no longer cuts it, even though (if it's designed well, in a unique way) I still think it's far more impressive than a fancy website. I have a website, but there is nothing on it other than a message that explains why I have no time to design it (because I would prefer to spend all my time and energy designing for real projects for real people). That's what works for me, at the moment, but I know that as more designers enter the industry, it's only going to become more challenging to think of something unique that can get you noticed.

## USING SOCIAL MEDIA

Social media, which involves interaction with users worldwide through the power of the Internet, has really blown the design industry apart.

Kevin Burr feels that social media has both positive and negative effects, which require that, as a promotional medium, it be treated with great care and caution:

> *The Internet and social media can be your best friend or your worst enemy. It's all*
> *about what you make of it. When you use the Internet and social media as a means*
> *to promote your business, you have to be very careful in what you say and how*
> *people perceive you. One wrong step, and the entire community knows about it. But*
> *if you remain approachable, offer good insight, and help others, your reputation can*
> *help generate more work.*

Everyone, and I mean everyone, has something to say. Whether it's important or interesting is another matter, but they'll do a good job of trying to get you to hear it. And that's perfectly fair. I'm not exactly sure whether social media has directly increased the number of designers in the world, but one thing is for certain: It makes you aware of just how many there are.

One interesting trend that I've noticed: The big agencies don't tweet or blog that much, mainly because they don't have to—they have their reputation to rely on. For smaller, independent companies and freelancers, the situation is different: Social media becomes an avenue for exposure—after all that's exactly what the vehicle of social media is: a cry for attention. Is this an advantage? Absolutely. Anything that creates connections among people can only be a good thing.

Stephanie Reeves understands that social media isn't the only route to securing a professional position but believes that it can only help:

> *Social media won't get anyone a job but I certainly don't think I could get the job I*
> *want without it. Again, it's about involvement; I think that employers want their new*

*blood to be aware of how social media can work. Being aware of recent advancements is one of the things that make young graduates so attractive to companies.*

*Sending your CV and printed portfolio with "I love your company" written on the back of your business card isn't enough anymore. Employers want to see that you have a genuine interest in your chosen field and the confidence to talk about it before they even get near to interviewing you. They do their homework and they want to see that you do yours. I can't see how blogs, social networks, and online portfolios could be a disadvantage unless you haven't got one.*

## BLOGGING FOR LEADS

The Internet grows every second of every day. It never sleeps. Since the mainstream became wise to search-engine optimization, and the practice of sharing design-related links through social media became a common practice, we've been inundated with often-pointless logo-design-related blog posts every day.

Steve Douglas coined the interesting term *logo-raiding*, which relates to this increasingly common tactic. I was lucky enough to ask him to share his thoughts on the subject:

> *Social media allows designers to get "out there." The problem is, there's an awful lot of designers trying to get "out there." And that's what leads to noise. As designers compete for clicks and traffic, they sometimes resort to pinching other designer's work—often without credit—and publishing posts that are little less than collections of other peoples' designs and labeling it "50 logos of cats." The noise can be very difficult to rise above, and quality material is often drowned out. When I first started on the Internet in the mid '90s, it was relatively easy to get decent search-engine placement for almost any designer willing to put in the time. It's not so easy any more. And getting less so every day.*

Think of this situation as fishing. The post or website is the net. They hook you in with the promise of showing you a bunch of logos, supposedly to inspire you for your own future works. Yet, underneath there is a shark at work that's only interested in Internet traffic. The more fish they get, the more successful that particular blog or website becomes.

Unfortunately, the practice of logo raiding is not just carried out by logo design inspiration websites or blogs, but by some designers themselves. This is perfectly fine as long as they're crediting the work and providing links to the designer of the logos that they choose to showcase. Not providing credit, however, can make it look like the posted logos are the work of the author of the blog post and could trick potential clients into thinking that that designer is of a higher experience or skill level than he or she actual is.

**Remember:** The ideal way to get traffic to your work is to do it the honest way—by creating outstanding solutions that you designed yourself.

283

## STAYING GROUNDED

The best form of promotion is to consistently create brilliant work. Even if you spend time and money getting your name out there, it won't be worthwhile unless it impresses potential clients.

When you begin to build a good reputation, it can be easy to let your ego take over and start thinking you're the best designer that has ever graced the earth. I believe that the great achievers in the world—and this is applicable to every type of profession—are those who have an extremely well-honed work ethic and don't rest on past achievements. The drive and focus to continually beat your previous achievements and conquer new goals is what keeps such people motivated. The beauty of designing logos is that each task poses a new problem to solve, so keeping the passion alive shouldn't be a problem.

## THE FUTURE OF LOGO DESIGN

So, where does this leave us? We could make a wild assumption that computers will take over our minds completely and design logos for us, in effect replacing the role of the designer completely. But that's unlikely to happen. I can only imagine that it will continue to evolve, with designers having to make even greater changes to keep up with the pace. With the recent global economic crisis, more and more designers are freelancing because of the decreasing number of design jobs available. I can't help but think that the Internet has also played a big role.

With social media becoming more and more prevalent in people's everyday personal and working lives, it would be closed-minded to predict that it isn't going to play an even bigger role not just in logo design but in the whole industry in the future. Even today, it's possible for teams to be put together without even having to meet face to face. That's very exciting from a collaboration standpoint, but I hope that the beauty of working within a team through immediate firsthand interaction doesn't disappear completely.

What about the distribution of clients? Will the massive firms continue to dominate and monopolize the jobs for the world's most popular brands? Probably, but maybe not. One thing is for certain: There will always be logos and the people who design them.

# Index

287

289